To a true Diva!
Happy adventuring
through life, Pam o
[signature]

Happy travels!
[signature]

MW01600585

For Keri
Yesterday, Today, Always

[THE MISSION]
Aliveness for All

"Don't ask what the world needs. Ask what makes you come alive and go do it. Because what the world needs is people who have come alive."

–Howard Thurman

Diving into aliveness has given us life.

This was true over 10 years ago when Evolution Through Vacation was simply the seed of an idea.

And it's still true today.

In fact, we're more inspired than ever to help even more people find their version of aliveness.

To taste the sweetness—and the pain. To savor real moments. To experience more of ourselves. To forge substantial connections with others. To make friends with the world. And to feel so freakin' grateful for it all.

We know you want it, too.

We know you've felt your heart stir at the words *what if?* The pull of your soul, longing to be seen. Your insides jumping at the idea that: *there still might be time to be who I really am.*

Most days, however?

Many of us dampen this inner fire.

We do our jobs, not honor our livelihood. We fulfill our obligations, not commit to our passions. We get through life, not truly live it.

In this pressure-filled world, this is understandable.

It can sometimes feel easier or safer or more manageable to just skim the surface instead of deep diving, to sleepwalk through it all on auto-pilot or, conversely, to fill each day with busywork and distractions to the brim so there's no chance to be reminded of what really matters to us.

Until we go on vacation.

Seriously, think about it.

Vacations free us.

They allow our innate desire for fun, lightness and exploration to show up.

They inspire us to let go, open up and live in the moment.

They encourage our true happiness to shine and our core self to glow.

Vacations show us what life is like when we're truly alive.

Jason Mraz sang, "You don't need a vacation when there's nothing to escape from."

As much as we dig Mr. A-Z and his avocado farm, we respectfully disagree.

That's because we see vacation differently.

The word's roots are in being *empty* and *free*; vacation gives us the chance to *empty and free* ourselves of things that weigh us down.

Not escape them for a while but, truly, release the grip of inner burdens.

Burdens like what? Here's a short list:

- Expectations
- Routines
- Judgments
- Stress
- Pressure
- Musts
- Can'ts
- Shoulds

Letting go of and surrendering all this weightiness opens space in our minds and hearts to move and evolve into our aliveness.

To fill that space with spirit fuel.

To listen for our deepest wishes.

To hear our inner wisdom.

To experience awe and wonder.

To play and laugh, dance and sing, breathe deeply and fully, relax and regroup.

And to experience this delicious existence called aliveness.

That's why we wrote *Evolution Through Vacation*.

And why we're more excited than ever to share it with you.

As a reminder that this possibility exists all the time. It's just simply easier to access on vacation.

So, why not start there?

To jog your memory.

To reconnect with your aliveness.

To hang 10 with the Universe.

And then? To bring it all back to real life. So that every day, truly, is a vacation day.

Doesn't that sound like a freakin' blast? Like the adventure, literally, of a lifetime?

For real, what else is there for us to do with this one trip we have?

Honestly, what better way to spend our lives than alive?

Seriously, pack your bags, friends.

It's time to go.

- Gretchen & Elissa

[INTRO]

[INTRO] It's About Vacation

The space between
Neither this
        nor that
Ripe, potent
        uncertain, shaky
A Dawning, a Dusking...
The immanent threshold
        emerging
crossing...to what?
        Slow down
The moment is calling you
to pay...exquisite...attention...

–Christine McDougall

Quick question: are you alive right now?

Not breathing and blinking and "Um-if-I-wasn't-how-could-I-be-reading-this-book?" kind of alive.

We mean, like, really alive? Alive in a space of total creation? On the edge of your seat and completely engaged? In the moment and open to all possibilities?

Think about it.

In today's world, for all too many of us, living an alive life doesn't always come easy.

Our sweet sense of glee gets buried by to-dos and tasks, expectations and obligations. Our wide-eyed sense of wonder gets squashed by should and shouldn't, can't and mustn't, do this and don't do that. Our innate aliveness gets crushed with the weight and toll of this thing called life.

Except...

Except when we extract ourselves from the spin-cycle and find some inspiration. When we break free from the day-to-day and find some excitement. When we take ourselves out of the routine, hit the road and find something new.

Yep, we come alive when we go on vacation.

It's true: Whether halfway around the world on a month-long adventure or a weekend visit to the next town over, exploring new places and experiences does something to us.

Vacation relaxes our brow and eases our tension.

Opens us up and allows us to be present.

Gives us access to an aliveness that's waiting inside us all, right under the surface.

Evolution Through Vacation helps you find it.

Sounds good. So, how does it work?

First things first:

Evolution Through Vacation or e>v ("e-through-v") isn't here to tell you where to go or what to do on your next trip. Again, it could be an adrenaline-filled excursion or a quiet getaway; where you go is not the point.

Instead, through thought-provoking questions and fun experiments, e>v ("e-through-v") encourages you to dive into your upcoming vacation with energy and intention, using the external world to discover more about your inner world.

Traveling with e>v encourages you to open your mind to new choices, your eyes to new viewpoints and your heart to new joys.

It invites you to empty yourself of everything from outdated habits to unconscious reactions.

It emboldens you to access the courage and grant yourself permission to open up to all that life is offering you.

And, for the long-haul, it cheers you on as you create a sustainable practice that rocks your world, shakes your core and changes your life from a day-to-day routine of simply living to a holistic experience of truly being alive.

All. The. Time.

How can vacation do all that?!

Part laboratory, part playground, vacation is the ultimate space in which to play with aliveness.

You visit new places, talk with new people, eat new foods, discover new facets of yourself.

You're in an ambiguous space; curiosity and surprise are available to you; the unfamiliar is all around.

You don't necessarily know what will happen next.

And on vacation, that's OK. In fact, that's often why you go!

It's in this state of traveling—of *liminality*—that the immense opportunity for exploration, inspiration and evolution is close at hand and utterly inviting.

Wait, wait, wait. Limi-*what?*

Liminality.

Found in anthropology and psychology, liminality refers to being on a threshold, in the middle, neither here nor there.

It's a concept rooted in transition: think airports, hotels, doorways, open windows, pilgrimages, festivals, at equinox and solstice, midnight, twilight, under the mistletoe, when you wake from sleep and can't tell if you were dreaming, in shape shifters, on the road, in the middle, in limbo, on vacation.

It's exploratory and delightfully unknown; it's present and uninhibited; it's open and expansive.

Liminality is a key component, idea and premise of the e>v way of life.

For example, think of the feeling you get when you're a day or two into vacation and you suddenly realize you are oh-so-free at that very moment: free from rules and regulations, free from expectations and the daily to-dos.

And, suddenly, a rush of giddiness fills your belly with warm fuzzies and fluttery butterflies and emotions indescribable.

And you feel like you could take on the world, hold it in your hand and flip it upside down all at the same time.

This is liminality.

Even cooler?

Exploring and experimenting in the space of liminality not only has the power to change *your* world, but it has the potential—as ecumenical teacher Richard Rohr sums up—to change the *entire* world.

Rohr says:

"(Liminality) is when we are betwixt and between, have left one room but not yet entered the next room, any hiatus between stages of life, stages of faith, jobs, loves, or relationships. It is that graced time when we are not certain or in control, when something genuinely new can happen... Much of the work of human destiny itself is to get people into liminal space and to keep them there long enough to learn something essential and genuinely new. It is the ultimate teachable space."

Now, that's what we're talkin' about.

In the open space of liminality—in betwixt and between, *on vacation*—we are free to discover what moves and inspires us, to remember who we really are, to create new realities and to step into our aliveness.

This is *Evolution Through Vacation*.

[INTRO] It's About You

But little by little,
as you left their voices behind,
the stars began to burn
through the sheets of clouds,
and there was a new voice
which you slowly
recognized as your own,
that kept you company
as you strode deeper and deeper
into the world, determined to do
the only thing you could do,
determined to save
the only life you could save.

—Mary Oliver

The next premise of *Evolution Through Vacation?*

At this very moment, within your being, you have the courage, creativity and capability to live your most fulfilling life. On your next vacation and, even better, every single day.

The glitch?

From a young age, the majority of us are taught to ignore this wisdom. To doubt this knowledge.

And, worst of all, to look outside ourselves for the truth.

Parents, teachers, experts, pundits, gurus. All these well-meaning (and sometimes not-so-well-meaning) channels pontificate on how we, male or female, athletes or artists, co-op members or corporate colleagues, should act or ought to feel.

Squashed under layers of expectations, obligations, habits. Steamrolled by an external need to be authenticated in some shape or form. Crushed so tight that half the time we can't tell whether we're feeling a deep-seated need to shake things up or we're just rumbling from the burrito we had at lunch. All in allegiance to fitting in, being accepted or finding validation in people other than ourselves.

And now?

After sitting through this lifelong course of limitation? After overpaying your blend-in-with-the-crowd dues? After following concrete rules for 20, 30, 50 or, even, 70 years?

You have full permission to leave it behind.

Ditch it. Toss it. Chuck those prescriptive directives to the side because, with e>v, you are now free to release your external-expert addiction and reconnect with your very own internal authority.

Yep, buried under the daily grind, the customs you've believed and, sometimes, the outright lies you've been sold, your all-knowing inner being, soul, spirit, vibe, core, essence, whatever-the-heck-you-want-to-call-it is there, waiting to be rediscovered.

And e>v is your search party.

In the chapters ahead, you'll learn how to use your next vacation—and those relaxed rules of liminality—to intentionally try things out and try things on.

To see past the clutter, listen for the whispers of your heart and unearth what really matters to you.

To celebrate your You-ness, to fly your freak flag and relish your unique genius.

To explore how to finally become the hero in this epic saga called your life.

At first, this may be hard to fully accept. You may say:

> • "Yeah, I hate my job. But I can't quit! I have bills to pay!"

> • "That's just the way things are. I can't do anything about it."

> • "No way! Insert-name-here would never allow me do that, be that, live that way."

Think again.

With e>v, you'll also learn that these statements, seemingly powerful and daunting as they are, are nothing but stories.

Stories that control your life in sneaky ways. Stories that sabotage and hijack what could be your utter and complete bliss. Stories you've inadvertently bought into after years of looking beyond your own self for answers.

Stories that you're choosing to recite and repeat day after day after day.

Yes, you can blame parents or partners, friends or foes, situations or society for frustration in life. But there comes a moment when you realize you are an active participant in the continuation of this reality.

No one is making you stay as you are.

No one is forcing you to pass up your dreams.

No one is standing in your way except you.

Sorry, not sorry, friend: Only you can write your own story.

No lie.

With e>v, you'll learn that you're living in a world of choice and you're choosing to behave the way you behave all the time.

With e>v, you'll learn that while you may experience adverse expectations from the world, you have the power to change the narrative.

With e>v, your outdated habits and excuses will get the boot and you'll learn that, in this universe, there's no space for placing blame. For pointing the finger. For waiting for someone else to change things for you. For sitting back and just accepting your lot. For being along for the ride. For talking yourself out of what's best for your heart, mind, body or soul.

NO.

Just no.

Look around: the most uplifting, enlightening and inspiring stories in all of human history are about people who figuratively—and sometimes literally— pushed back on living in a way that was painful, unsatisfactory or unfair to themselves and, at times, entire populations of people.

This is your invitation to take your place. To lead your life. To write your story.

With e>v, you are the Editor-in-Chief. And you have a big red pen in your hand, ready to make all the changes you want.

To change things if you're unhappy or dissatisfied or bored or angry or fed up.

To alter what you believe, what you do, where and with whom you dedicate your energy.

To remember and re-discover yourself; to grant permission for enlightened appreciation of different possibilities; to feel alive starting from this day forward.

As Yung Pueblo says, "Allow yourself to transform as many times as you need to be happy and free."

You are the one you've been waiting for.

You are the only You that will ever live in this space and time.

You were born to do this. Here. Now.

Practice it on vacation. Live it in life.

***Evolution Through Vacation* will show you how.**

[INTRO] It's About the Journey

"Leave the beaten track occasionally and dive into the woods. Every time you do so you will be certain to find something that you have never seen before. Follow it up, explore all around it and before you know it, you will have something worth thinking about to occupy your mind."

–Alexander Graham Bell

The final, core idea of e>v?

Every travel experience you have—from your next jaunt with your besties to a family adventure to a solo getaway—follows a path we all know well:

1) Preparation:
Planning, packing, getting ready to go

2) The Trip:
Traveling, touring, exploring your chosen destination

3) Re-Entry:
Sliding back into your life when you return

Sound familiar?

This well-worn path is a *Rite of Passage*.

Lots of interesting folks have explored this concept from big-thinking anthropologist Arnold van Gennep to that rad *Hero's Journey* philosopher Joseph Campbell to, now, you. (Side note: In addition to travel, experiences like birth, death, puberty, graduation and marriage are just some of the other transitions that Rites of Passage mark.)

One of the coolest things about it?

Most people who accept the quest of a Rite of Passage do so by choice, fully engage in the journey and, therefore, come out the other side eternally changed and utterly inspired. Moving through life in a whole new way, approaching new challenges with new perspectives.

That's what you're about to do with e>v.

You'll follow the three simple stages of a Rite of Passage—which beautifully mirror your evolution through your vacation. Here's how.

1) Preparation

"Become a possibilitarian." —Norman Vincent Peale

The first leg of your e>v adventure and the next section in this book is called Preparation or Prep.

For you research hounds out there, van Gennep called this step *Separation,* the preliminary space of travel where a seeker prepares to move from one place to another.

With e>v, Prep is a bit of metaphysical pondering, planning and list making.

It's taking stock of where you are with the knowledge that something new is coming 'round the bend.

It's pondering what you're moving away from and what you're moving toward.

It's preparing to go, inside and out.

Many spiritual guides living and passed, Wayne Dyer in particular, have talked about the idea: "as you think, so shall you be."

Prep poses questions to help you uncover who you want to be on the road and beyond, like:

  • **What will make this vacation different?**
  • **What could happen that would be brilliant in my eyes?**
  • **What habits or reactions stand in the way of these dreams?**
  • **What would this trip be like if I left those excuses behind?**
  • **What do I want to create?**

In short, Prep helps you rally your thoughts, uncover hidden stories, center your choices and solidify your intentions. All to manifest something magnificent in the next stage, the Trip!

2) The Trip

"Don't be timid and squeamish about your actions. All life is an experiment. The more experiments you make, the better." –Ralph Waldo Emerson

And you're off!

You're now entering the juicy space without firm definition, that place ripe for exploration and evolution. Van Gennep actually called this stage *Liminality,* the cool idea we just talked about meaning "betwixt and between."

***Evolution Through Vacation* calls this phase of exploration the Trip.**

From your intentions created in Prep, the Trip now equips you with ideas, tools and tips to choose your perspectives and actions in order to bring your ideal vision to life.

When you are here—on your Trip, on vacation—everything is bursting with possibility.

The Trip helps you get closer to this magical moment with experiments that ask you what you want to do while on vacation:

> **• Do you want to get closer with yourself or others in your midst?**
> **• Do you want to step out of roles you've created and into others that energize you?**
> **• Do you want to experience life in a way that, right now, you can only imagine?**
> **• Who have you decided to be and what will you now do to make it so?**
> **• How can you stay in the moment and in liminality?**

In the Trip, you come face to face with these answers.

Then you learn how to put them in action, in the moment.

In the way only you can.

3) Re-Entry

"The most authentic thing about us is our capacity to create, to overcome, to endure, to transform, to love and to be greater than our suffering." –Ben Okri

Finally, the third stage in a Rite of Passage is akin to coming home.

Van Gennep referred to this as *Incorporation*, where the seeker integrates back into society.

Evolution Through Vacation calls this Re-Entry, where the traveler returns from whence they came.

Re-Entry recalls the insights and learning from your vacation and asks you what impact it will have on your daily existence. It presents ideas on how to incorporate the energy from The Trip into your life in order to feel more alive than ever. It offers experiments to help you take on a "warrior's attitude to discomfort," as Pema Chödrön says, all to transform your life into a "path of awakening." It equips you to live what you have learned and keep these learnings present from this moment on.

Re-Entry asks:

- **What looks different in your life now, having seen and experienced all that you did?**
- **Where do you see aliveness around you now?**
- **What will keep that sense of aliveness with you?**
- **What's next?**

Re-Entry offers tools to transform how you view coming back to your life after a wonderful, amazing vacation. It helps you realize how easy and necessary it is to integrate all the amazing discoveries you've found on the road. And, in the spirit of choice, it asks what's next on your personal journey and allows you to define it your way.

In short, this is where your vacation energy becomes everyday energy.

This is where you stay *alive*.

NAV TIP: INTRO TO *NAV TIPS*

One last note before you hit the road: throughout the book you'll find e>v *Navigation Tips,* or *Nav Tips.*

These are additional insights and prompts on the topic just discussed or questions and queries to get you thinking about your own personal life in context of the ideas presented.

Here's our first Nav Tip for what you're reading right now:

• If you have a printed copy of the e>v book, grab a pen or pencil and mark it up.

• If you have an e-version, we encourage you to get a dedicated e>v journal or notebook for all your musings.

Yes, you can do the experiments and answer the questions in your head. And you'll be amazed at how you will change over the course of this adventure.

Because of this, it's really fun to look back at your ideas and thoughts throughout your journey to see, in your own words, just how far you've come.

In addition, you'll most likely have side thoughts, ideas, impressions or feelings about your experience through this process: everything from your emotions to the weather to your a-ha moment to the most memorable conversation to the most hilarious quote to... you get the picture.

All in all, capturing the cool stuff as it happens will add to and help conjure up your e>v context as you move through your experience and, especially, upon Re-Entry.

Use these pages in a way that will serve you as you do this vacation differently. Some ideas:

- **Choose to doodle, draw, scribble or sketch**
- **Make simple lists of sites, things, people or signs that moved you in some way**
- **Note random (and important) sounds, colors, sights or smells**
- **Collect tickets, maps, menus, leaves, coasters**
- **Go beyond landscapes and capture the spirit of your day in photos, video, audio**
- **Gather pages of local magazines, newspapers**
- **Pull out e>v experiments as fun conversation starters with your travel mates or new people you meet along the way to expand the discussion**
- **Co-create something with the world around you!**

So, you ready to go?

To get started, to explore, to engage and, most of all, to have fun?

Remember: this is your life.

This is your journey.

This is your chance to feel alive.

Now, get out there and explore.

Bon Voyage!

[PREP]

[PREP] Welcome

"In the garden of gentle sanity, may you be bombarded by coconuts of wakefulness."

–Chögyam Trungpa Rinpoche

Welcome to Prep.

The expansive space where you create your vacation.

So: What do you want to create?

As with any trip, prepping and getting ready stirs up many thoughts and emotions: anticipation, hope, giddiness, excitement, fear, anxiety, you name it!

To engage, explore and expand these feelings, Prep is a space for you to plan, play, ponder and, you got it, prepare.

All to get to the bottom of quandaries like:

> **• What are the stories you're packing into this trip even before going the first mile?**
> **• What will you take along?**
> **• And, more importantly, what are you willing to leave behind?**
> **• Who do you want to be on this vacation?**
> **• What do you want to learn on the road?**
> **• What do you want to create on this adventure?**
> **• How might this vacation be different from any other before?**

This is your space to muse over how this adventure will be unique.

This is your time to dive in and dig deep.

This is your place to plan for something incredible.

And, as always, this is your process and you will not be graded or judged by anyone. Including yourself!

One more time: This is all about you.

You write your story.

You create your vacation.

You choose your own adventure. Always.

So, let's get pepped for Prep!

[PREP] Check Your Baggage

"We do not grow absolutely, chronologically. We grow sometimes in one dimension, and not in another; unevenly. We grow partially. We are relative. We are mature in one realm, childish in another. The past, present & future mingle and pull us backward, forward, or fix us in the present. We are made up of layers, cells, constellations."

–Anaïs Nin

(En)Lighten Your Load.

Welcome to Experiment Number One on your fabulous e>v adventure.

This first one's a biggie, so grab a beverage, find a chair, settle in, open up and let's rock.

Because, it's time to Check Your Baggage.

As you probably guessed, we're not talking about that roller bag you lug to and fro.

Nope. This is the *internal* kind of baggage. The unconscious crud that trips you up. The emotional sludge that weighs you down. The heavy-as-lead crap you pack on every single vacation that deserves the boot.

The stuff we're talking about?

> **• Outdated ideas that stand in the way of
> your evolution on this trip**
> **• The auto-tales you've been telling about
> your life as you presently know it**
> **• The strict script you've been living by**
> **• The limited view of what you've come to
> expect from the world around you**
> **• In short: the stories of your very existence**

The stories that keep you safe and comfortable. And stuck in the same-old, same-old.

The stories that tell you that the known may suck, but the unknown could bring something even suckier.

The stories that convince you that things aren't happening for you in the way you envisioned because you're doing something wrong.

Or that there's something wrong with you.

Or that you're not really worthy of ever being happy on any level in your life.

At all.

Ever.

STOP. RIGHT. THERE.

We all have ruts we've created (stories) and deeply entrenched habits (more stories) that help us forget that we have choices. We all have defenses (stories) and automatic reactions (more stories) that stand in the way of our evolution.

Some stories were true once and no longer are.

Some stories were told by others and we believed them.

Some stories were learned from the media or magazines or movies or TV.

Some stories were born out of fear or protection.

Some stories have enlightened us in some way over the years, and many stories have been a serious dimmer switch on our radiance.

The point?

These stories and all their weight make up your baggage.

And in this experiment—and on this vacation—it's time to reconsider this baggage and the stories packed within.

On this trip, it's time to ask yourself:

"Self, what is the story I want to write? What are the strengths I really want to take with me? What beliefs, judgments, even items or articles deserve to be left behind? Which would be irritating stowaways? And what am I going to do about it?"

Because, like it or not, these stories will tag along with you on your upcoming vacation—and right back home again—unless you decide to open that inner suitcase and confront your baggage head on.

So, let's do it.

Let's Check Your Baggage.

First, Unlock the Junk in the Trunk:

Yep, you gotta I.D. it to free it, so name your baggage.

Detail it. Be specific. Be ruthless. Get to the bottom of this trunk-o-crud and see what you find.

Even if it's oogy, even if it's grimy, you can handle it. In fact, you'll be glad you did.

Jot down ideas here or in your journal about the following.

What I've hauled along on past trips that weighed me down or wasn't useful:

What I think I *should* bring or who I think I *should* be on this trip:

   • **Note:** should is a word to consider leaving behind; should is often an alert that guilt is nearby! (Sooo, stop "shoulding" all over yourself!)

Who or what I'll bravely leave behind this time instead:

• Consider unproductive baggage like assuming the worst: "My luck, it'll rain the whole time." **What doubts do you carry from past experience?**

• Maybe it's subconscious baggage: "Work will be so busy when I get back." **What do you pack that stands in the way of being present?**

• And then, there's that dang *should*: "I should stay at my parent's / in-law's / XYZ's house instead of getting a hotel." **What shoulds might you be packing again and again?**

———

NAV TIP: STUCK GETTING UN-STUCK?

Before you can pack something new, it's useful to be free of the old. And sometimes, that can be a friggin' challenge. To say the least.

Resistance to naming or releasing baggage is an important noticing, too.

Sometimes, simply noticing resistances that pop up diminishes the power of baggage. That in itself creates space for something different.

Other times, it's enough to just explore what you can, go with the flow, remove judgment from the process and see what happens. Just like you don't experience your entire vacation the first day, this, too, is a process. **Play with it.**

———

Next, Pack Something New:

Find some outdated stories in your baggage? Chucked 'em by the side of the road? Cool.

Now, it's time to pack anew. Or: it's one step to ditch what doesn't serve you. It's a second step to clarify what will take its place.

Why? Simple quantum physics. (Really.)

Yep, quantum physics—that mind-bending scientific field—reminds us that nature doesn't like a vacuum; if you give it a void, it will suck in whatever it can to fill the empty space.

Same goes for your subconscious.

Once you've cleared out old stories and created some space, your brain will latch on to all sorts of stuff you had no idea you were pondering if you don't make new choices consciously.

So, let's fill that space with some enlightened intentions.

As the form and focus you give your thoughts, intentions are all about what you want to create, who you want to be and how you want to live. They convey what you want in a way that offers energy and excitement. And they're super-powerful when they're pure and baggage-free.

Because, news flash, intentions don't get along with stories. At all.

Or: when setting intentions, this ain't no space to disguise *don't wants* (baggage) as *wants* (intentions).

Example:

"I don't want to stay in a crappy hotel" doesn't tell anyone, including you, what you do want.

- "I don't want to stay in a crappy hotel" simply regurgitates your belief—your baggage—that you've seen evidence of crappy hotels in the past, thus hotels have the possibility to be crappy in the future. Hence, your intention and, therefore, your experience is centered on the baggage of exactly what you don't want: crappy hotels.

Instead: stating things like "I want first-class service" or "I want upgrades at every turn" or "I want to be treated like royalty" clarifies what you do want in a hotel experience.

- These intentions are focused on what you believe is possible in a hotel experience. Hence, your intentions and what you experience is centered on what you actually want when seeking your next hotel experience.

In short, attention is the energy you give to your intentions.

And the more intense the attention, the more powerful the intention.

And it's up to you to ensure you're giving the most beneficial attention to your most powerfully ideal intention.

You dig?

NAV TIP: WHERE'S YOUR ATTENTION?

It ain't rocket science. The simple adage says it best: "Where your attention goes, the energy flows."

So, where's your attention? What type and level of energy will you have for your intentions?

Play with these questions and get ready to create some magic.

My most fabulous self on this trip looks like... Centered? Sassy? Brave? All-out wonderful?

I will create the best trip ever as I... Step into my freakin' magnificence? My incredible worthiness? My ME-ness?

What I dare to bring along with me this time is... A secret desire to sing with the street musicians? The question I've always wanted to ask my travel mate? A level of bravery that I've only yet seen a glimpse of?

I'll display my commitment to my intention through... Thoughtfulness? Grace? Humility?

Think big and jot down your own ideas here or in your journal.

[PREP] Map It Out

"All the freaky people make the beauty of the world."

–Michael Franti

Journey to the world within.

So far, we've talked baggage and intentions for your upcoming trip. Cool stuff, indeed.

Now, armed with this new knowledge and steeped in possibility, it's the perfect time to take a peek into your life as a whole and how your upcoming trip can offer new insight and perspectives on your entire existence.

Welcome to the e>v Life Map.

The e>v Life Map offers you perspective on your own personal geography—your life experience—right here and now.

It helps you define who you are and where you're at.

It helps you see what's present so you can identify what's great and not-so-great.

It helps you uncover and release even more baggage and set even deeper intentions for this trip and your life.

And, OMG, it's fun. :)

————

NAV TIP: CHOICE IS EVERYWHERE

As you work through the Life Map, do it your way. Base it on your everyday existence, the itinerary for your trip, the things you want to ponder while you are away. Whatever your little heart desires.

————

1) You Gotta Know Where You Are To Know Where You're Going:

First up, as we discussed, vacations are a playground. They push us out of our everyday existence and allow us to step into new possibilities; they help us see and feel evidence of freedom and fun; they help us imagine a life where everything, on a scale from 1 to 10, is 100!

So, to start playing with this concept in a tangible, real-world way, consider each of these seven Life Areas, inspired by Julia Cameron, author of *The Artist's Way*.

Health / Stuff / Play / Relationships
Expression / Purpose / Spirit

To e>v, these are the areas that matter the most; the places where we set our goals and objectives; the spaces where we hope to see and feel the best.

Breathe them in, read through the descriptions, ponder the questions, feel your reactions starting to bubble up in your body and get ready to (r)evolutionize your world.

Health:
What's your sense about the skin you're livin' in? Feeling strong? Vibrant? Mucky? Yucky? What unhelpful stories do you tell about your health?

Stuff:
What do you surround yourself with? What's important to you materially? And, what makes these things important? Be mindful of old stories that might pop for you here.

Play:
Where do you find laughter and joy? What eases tension, releases stress, introduces calm and balance? What's your baggage about what play means to you?

Relationships:
Where do love and compassion show up in your life? What beliefs do you have that help you build relationships? What expectations stands in your way?

Expression:
Where does your creativity shine through? How do you express yourself in the world? What are your stories about what it means to be creative?

Purpose:
What gifts do you have to share with the world? Are you doing what you love and loving what you do? When do you feel like you are in total flow? Or not?

Spirit:
Where do you seek insights on life's big questions? About your place in the universe, your relation to a higher being, your connection with everything else? What stories exist for you here?

Understand the seven Life Areas? Cool.

Now ask yourself:

What's your *Level of Aliveness* (LOA) in each?

How excited and enthused are you by your life in each of these spaces?

How are each of these Life Areas grooving or grumbling?

Which are light as a feather and which are laden with baggage to the nth?

Let's find out.

On the good 'ol scale of 1-10 (10 = blissed out), assign a number to each Life Area based on your current Level of Aliveness (LOA). How you're feeling right now. Today. This minute.

Don't think too hard, just go with your gut and jot down your number here or in your journal.

Health:_____

Stuff:_____

Play:_____

Relationships:_____

Expression:_____

Purpose:_____

Spirit:_____

2) Explore Further:

Rated your LOA in the seven life areas? Awesome. Next, step back and ponder a bit. Jot down any and all thoughts, feelings or sensations that pop up about each Life Area in response to these questions:

• What does your life look like in each of the Life Areas in this moment?
• What's working for you? And what's the baggage that you're carrying around?
• How familiar is this terrain? What's known? What's unknown?

Health:

Stuff:

Play:

Relationships:

Expression:

Purpose:

Spirit:

3) Discover Your Personal Geography:

Next up? There are seven Life Areas and seven continents. (Coincidence? We think not.)

Without thinking too hard about it, place one of the seven Life Areas (Health, Stuff, Play, Relationships, Expression, Purpose, Spirit) and your "Level of Aliveness" (LOA) number on each of the seven continents below. Or make a list in your journal and pair up a continent with a Life Area and LOA number.

Why? We'll get to that! For now, just trust the experiment. And yourself!

Have at it. We'll wait.

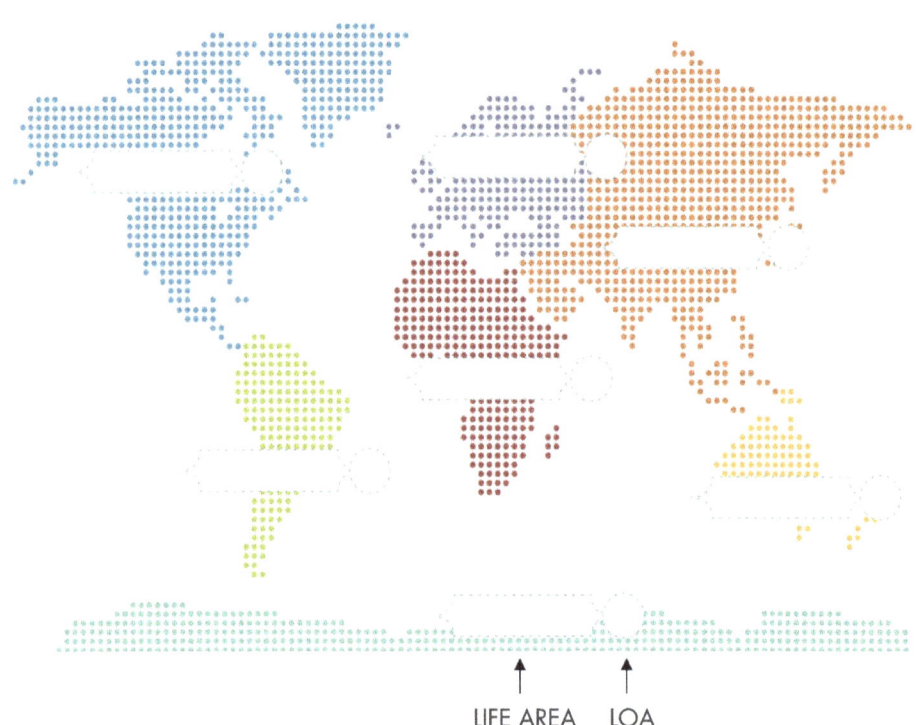

LIFE AREA   LOA

4) Explore Even Further:

OK, what's new about these Life Areas now that you've plotted them on the map? Do you see anything that you didn't before? What does the map add to how you feel about the Life Area? Or the LOA number you gave it? Play with these questions for added insights:

Jot down 3-5 words that describe the connection between the continent you chose for each Life Area and the Life Area itself.

What do these words say about your beauty? Your baggage? Your aliveness?

5) Meet Your Hot Spots:

Finally, look at your Life Map one last time. Which three Life Areas / continents grab your attention the most? Or: what are the *Hot Spots* in your life that are calling for you? Write them here or in your journal. Be sure to include any thoughts about the locale too!

Hot Spot #1:

Hot Spot #2:

Hot Spot #3:

And congratulations!

You've just completed your Life Map and identified your Hot Spots for this trip.

This Life Map and, especially, these Hot Spots will come up a lot as you play with e>v so keep them top of mind.

These are the emotional spaces that will get your attention when you're on the road.

These are the metaphorical places you'll explore with all the upcoming, in-the-moment experiments ahead in The Trip.

Rock on.

NAV TIP: NO PRESSURE

Don't worry, these Hot Spots might change along your journey.

And, you can pick new ones on your next adventure.

Or try something else tomorrow. Or even later today.

No pressure on vacation, remember?

For now, sit with these and get ready to keep learning.

[PREP] Grrr-Attitude

"You are imperfect, you are wired for struggle, but you are worthy of love and belonging."

–Brené Brown

Thanks for everything.

You've dug deep, learned some things about yourself, determined what parts of your life are jiving and, more importantly, which parts of your life are making you stand up and take notice.

And now, you're ready for the next step in your e>v journey: giving thanks.

Author Melody Beattie tells us, "Gratitude unlocks the fullness of life." And e>v wholeheartedly agrees.

So, to begin this experiment, look to the three Hot Spots you've just identified. Think about how these Hot Spots make you feel and, even if you gave them a '1' on the LOA scale, take notice of what you are thankful for in those areas right this minute.

Yep, take notice of your gratitude.

Celebrate what is working.

What is cool.

What does make you smile.

There are always magnificent gifts hiding in every challenge; there are always noteworthy aspects that often get the humble-mumble when we're analyzing our lives.

In this experiment, it's time to shake off that old notion that it's bad or wrong or obnoxious to appreciate and acknowledge your goodness. (As you now know, that's nothing but a story anyway!)

Instead, embrace your obnoxious gratitude.

Open up to it, feel it to your toes, in your bones, through your entire being as you embrace your beauty, your values, your talents, your strengths.

And, in the biggest, loudest way that you know how, show your gratitude here or in your journal:

What do you appreciate about your 3 Hot Spots at this very moment?

What are some compliments you receive from others about your 3 Hot Spots?

In your 3 Hot Spots, who are you when no one's looking?

Finish this sentence: "My 3 Hot Spots are kick-ass because…"

Is there anything from this list that you'd like to add to your Hot Spots? Or your Life Map as a whole? Do it now!

[PREP] Be. Do. Know.

"Prepare your mind to receive the best that life has to offer."

–Ernest Holmes

As we move into the final experiment in Prep, all we can say is: awesome. Like in the true sense of the word.

You've faced some tough stuff. And now, equipped with your Hot Spots, you have some meaningful, internal places to explore as you journey around your external world.

So, what's next?

Ah yes, a little experiment that reveals how you'll soon begin to access your new level of aliveness on the road. A little phrase that holds the key to unlocking your inner super power. A little thing known as the e>v magic spell.

Be. Do. Know.

Three little words, infinite possibility.

Individually, in a random sequence, these words—Be, Do, Know—are basic. Used with intention and, most importantly, in this order, they are magic. Applied mindfully, these words will set you up for discoveries and sustainability throughout your adventure and beyond. **Here's how they work.**

1) Be:

From elite athletes to progressive business execs to Dorothy in the *Wizard of Oz*, the power of vision—imagining what you want and believing it to your core—has long been recognized as a force to be reckoned with.

So, what does this have to do with you?

As A.C. Ping penned in his book, *Be,* (yes, there's an incredible little book devoted entirely to this topic):

"If some of us can do amazing things, then ALL of us can do amazing things. In essence, you are what you believe."

The short and sweet? Being is anchored in your vision and your beliefs.

Yep, your power of vision is just as potent and magnetic as those folks mentioned above. Your beliefs have the strength and capacity to change what happens around you every moment. And your inner wisdom holds the key to every single thing you experience, starting on this vacation.

Heard this all before? Maybe not.

Big thinkers like scientist-spiritualist Gregg Braden have examined scientific evidence that proves our belief actually transforms things that occur within and around us.

As Braden says, "Simply by changing what we believe, we not only change the way we feel on the inside but we literally change the atoms—the stuff our world is made of—on the outside."

Or: we actually change the electrical and magnetic fields around us to respond in kind to the energy of our beliefs.

Whoa.

So, let's bring it to life. As you play with your three Hot Spots, check out these *being* games and see what opens up for you.

Name It:

Imagine the energy you want to bring to your Hot Spot, who you want to be in this very moment and on the road. Choose qualities you admire: VIP, Blissed Out & Centered, Daring Adventurer, Gentle Spirit, etc. Or personify it: Mountain Climber, Queen, Rock Star, etc. **Write them here or in your journal:**

Feel It:

With all your senses, take on what that being would feel. Don't be shy here. Feel it in your core, in your bones and yes, even in your atoms. What kinds of emotions or qualities does it stir up? What do you notice about being in this energy completely and truly? **Jot down noticings here:**

Embody It:

Get this being in motion. Sit in this being. Walk around in this being, talk like this being, hold your head up high in this being. It is You! Feel silly? Why? **Notice any resistances you have. What's holding you back?**

Mark It:

Put in a pin in this energy and this being. Right here and now. Examine your three Hot Spots through the eyes of this new being. What's new, different or transformed? What do the hot spots look like now? How can you practice this as you move forward in Prep? **Take note here or in your journal.**

NAV TIP: THIS AIN'T NO ACT

This experiment is not about role-playing so much as it is about remembering. Because, as you know, all the daring and caring, love and sass, confidence and calm—all of the being-ness you are conjuring here—is YOU. The real you. The who-you-really-are-you.

While you're playing with these new approaches and new energy, you are simply calling forth different parts of yourself. Perhaps even brushing off dusty aspects that you have not allowed out in years. **Welcome back, You.**

2) Do:

Next, as the same athletes and execs we mentioned become who they are, they believe in this being so strongly that they are guided to do the very thing that will bring them success.

Or, their being guides their doing.

Effortless. In flow. When a person is so moved by their belief that it appears they're not even trying, they're simply doing. Without questions, without hesitation, without fear.

As our friend Yoda says: "Do, or do not. There is no try." Or as e>v says: Once you are being magic, you do magic. Simple as that.

Let's give it a whirl.

Get back in your being space. You there? OK: Re-breathe in your being, stand in your being, walk around in your being, speak from your being.

Now, let your being guide your doing. As you continue through Prep, ask yourself, "If I acted from my being space, what would people see or experience of me?" For instance, how would a Daring Adventurer act as they planned their upcoming vacation or played with their Hot Spots? What would they do?

Finally, what are you noticing about the choices you have now? What's different from what you've experienced before? Could this be where the connection between being and doing is starting to really make sense and—ta daa!—you realize that it IS all up to you? Read on. It just might be!

3) Know:

Way to go.

You've got it going on. You're strutting your stuff and allowing your being to guide your doing. You've manifested an internal reality that is proving just how connected you are to yourself, to others, the world and the universe.

Really. Take a pause to notice, to reflect, to see the learnings, to feel the impact. All this makes up what you now know.

Or:

Once you see for yourself that your being creates your doing, you'll also soon see evidence of a new reality. And you'll *know* just how powerfully connected your choices are with absolutely everything you experience.

You'll start to understand that nothing just happens to you.

You'll start to understand that, instead, you're in charge of your happiness.

Even more, you'll start to understand that you can affect what goes on around you.

As Debbie Ford once said, when you shift your lens from "I'm IN the world" to "I AM the world," you'll start to understand that your choices—your being and your doing—literally transform the very world around you into what you know to be true.

This is Be, Do, Know at its core. And you now have the power to realize it.

Final step?

Consider these questions and possibilities to seal the deal.

From experimenting and playing with being and doing, what do you now know?

Check-in with yourself on new insights, new thoughts, interactions, energy level. What feels on? Off? In-between?

What the heck is going on here? What do you love about it? And, what freaks you out a little bit?! Feel it all. Jot it down.

NAV TIP: CYNIC ALERT

Aaaaand, even if you're pondering this in the slightest, don't try to pull a fast one on yourself with:

"Actually, I work best if I KNOW the right decision to make; then I'll DO it; and then I'll BE happy."

Really? The desire to know the right answer before taking any action is a story of the highest order. In fact, a need-to-know-first attitude will paralyze you because it forces you to:

• Make predictions based on a false reality (a.k.a. the future)
• Calculate every move carefully (a.k.a. manipulate)
• Control all the moving parts (a.k.a. play god)

Two likely results?

1. This saves you from wrong decisions or actions by encouraging you to do nothing at all.
2. Or, this puts you on a hamster wheel that keeps you chasing—yet never attaining—true happiness.

Instead, remember: Be. Do. Know.

Or, as Mr. Kobi Yamada says: "Sometimes you have to take the leap and build your wings on the way down." Trust that. **Even more, trust yourself.**

_____

[PREP] Final Prep Talk

"To travel is to take a journey into yourself."

–Danny Kaye

You've just taken a journey before even leaving home. Nice.

Now it's time for a few final thoughts to recap all the incredible learning you've just uncovered and unleashed. All to help solidify and sanctify your amazing aliveness. All to send you off in serious style.

So, remember:

- **Vacation = Play. This is about aliveness after all!**

- **You now have your permission to do what serves you deeply and best. Period.**

- **There is no RIGHT way or WRONG way. Your journey will not look like anyone else's. You're totally unique. How cool is that?**

- **Give yourself the gift of gratitude, often and obnoxiously.**

- **And finally, always remember: no matter where you go, there YOU are. Your being, your doing and your knowing are directly linked to YOUR choices. Right on.**

Now, let's hit the road.

[THE TRIP]

[THE TRIP] On the Verge

"Life is about not knowing, having to change, taking the moment and making the best of it, without knowing what's going to happen next. Delicious ambiguity."

–Gilda Radner

OMG, it's The Trip. And you. Are. Officially. On. Vacation.

Open up to opportunity and get ready to find your adventure because you've arrived!

It's the glee-filled, expansive, open-ended, brilliant space of exploration and fun. It's the possibility-packed, intention-intense rollercoaster of adventure. It's what being alive is all about: letting go, feeling good, smiling at strangers, exploring our planet.

Because, one more time for emphasis:

You! Are! On! Vacation!

We don't know what you'll find here; we do know it will be amazing. We do know the feeling of the butterflies. We do know how courageous you are. And we do know about the silly grin you have in anticipation of the wonders that await you. As Gilda said, it's "delicious ambiguity."

No matter what, as always, explore in the way that brings you to life in the present moment. In the way that honors your exploration. Your Trip!

Start your journey here.

You made it: you are now in that luscious space endearingly known as liminality—that wonderful space of betwixt and between.

Remember liminality?

The energy of aliveness.

While Arnold van Gennep coined the term, also-amazing anthropologist Victor Turner further developed the concept from being "in the middle" or "in transition" to suggest a time and space that's actually moldable and malleable.

Ready to be shaped by you.

On your journey, this liminal space is all around, through and through, ripe for exploration and evolution.

It's where old rules fall off and new possibilities appear.

It's a freeing space of pure creation.

And, best of all, it's yours.

So dive into it with the experiments ahead—playful invitations to shape this flexible space.

Step into this enchantment.

Jump into this liminality.

Leap into your aliveness and see what unfolds!

NAV TIP: HOW TO GET THE MOST OUT OF THE TRIP SECTION

Every day on your vacation—aka, on your Trip!—play with the following experiments, exercises and games in this section during the morning, day and evening and then hit repeat the next day.

Some games and experiments will become second nature; and you may want to revisit others for some in-the-moment aliveness tips and tricks.

All in all, this section is meant to equip you with fun ideas and goodies to do on your own or with your travel partners.

Or with the new friends you meet at the bar or concert or in the museum or wherever.

Even more, as you play with these ideas over the course of your vacation, see what changes, see what stays the same and where you fit in!

And—because it IS vacation, after all—have fun!

[THE TRIP] Checking In

"There is an old Tibetan saying: wherever you feel at home, you are at home. If your surroundings are pleasant, you are at home."

—The Dalai Lama

Let the games begin.

OK. So, you're reacquainted with liminality, you're awake and aware of everything around you, you're on the Trip, and now: it's time to check in.

Naturally, on your various and assorted travels, you won't always be staying in a hotel. No matter.

The idea of checking in still remains one of the first milestones of a vacation. It stands as an entrance to a new kind of world and experience.

So, let's kick things off and rev things up.

From your new surroundings to yourself, let's check in.

1) Feel It: Check In With Yourself

Remember, first and foremost, it's all about you. And, if you're like others, it can sometimes take a moment to fully transition into vacation mode.

Stopping to center yourself helps to connect with the present moment and allows you to release any residual stress you've inadvertently carried along en route. (Think Olympic diver: there's always the moment of pause before they take the plunge.)

To settle into your Trip, give this a try:

Set down your bags and belongings. Sit for a minute with your feet flat on the floor and your hands on your thighs, palms up or down, whatever is more comfortable for you.

Now, become quiet, close your eyes and simply notice how you feel. Are you breathing fast or slow? Are you tired? Excited? Giddy? Anxious? What's here? Feel it throughout your body for 30 seconds or so. Then:

Breathe In
Through your nose, inhale a deep breath for a count of 1, 2, 3, 4, 5 and hold briefly.

Breathe Out
Next, exhale through your nose and drop your shoulders, allowing the rest of your body to relax as you let go of any tension.

Breathe In
Through your nose, take another deep inhale for a count of 5 and breathe in all the feelings that will serve you on this vacation. Courage? Love? A sense of adventure? Hope?

Breathe Out
Finally, through your mouth, exhale a sigh of gratitude and give your whole being a chance to be thankful for the here and now.

And, welcome to your Trip.

———

This breathing pattern can help center you anytime, anywhere. So put it in your pocket. Practice when needed. Repeat as necessary.

———

2) Own it: Check In With Your Home Base

Next, it's time to move into your liminal home!

Whether you're in a five-star hotel, a shared-bathroom hostel, an apartment rental, a tent or guest room, the perfect way to move into your e>v Trip is to make this space truly yours for as long as you'll be here.

Remember: it's your space. So, make it yours.

No matter where you are, simply ask yourself:

- What type of space will reflect this journey?
- What's the mood?
- A retreat to rejuvenate in betwixt and between all your learnings? A refuge to release all your fears? A party space to keep the adventure alive?

Play with these questions, then explore the following ideas to get you moving in!

Unpack:

• Actually use the drawers and closet and hide your suitcase away. Um, that's what they're there for, right?

Amp it up:

• Energize the chi—from the Chinese: *spiritual energy*—of your room or space
• Turn on some music and shake your booty; you know you got it in ya
• Jump on the bed, be a kid; go ahead, no one's watching
• Make some noise and kick out the jams

Or, slow it down:

• Remember, there are no rules that say you have to hit the ground running
• Light a candle and draw a bath, alone or with a partner
• Put on the bathrobe, order room service and lounge; again, alone or with a partner
• Crawl under the covers for a quick catnap
• Put on your headphones and chill, baby, chill
• Meditate, stretch, do some yoga

Transform your space:

• Hate that bedspread? Fold it up and shove it in the closet.
• Can't stand the art? Put up your own maps or photos or posters or stuff you find along the way.
• Open the shades, or keep them closed
• Use lipstick or a bar of soap to write an intention on the mirrors or windows
• Cover the TV with a scarf—or more art!—to remove the distraction
• Screw in a colored light bulb; create a groovy vibe for late-night parties
• Spritz your favorite scent to clear the air
• Get all your senses going

Perhaps you're out in nature:
- Create mobiles and sculptures out of driftwood and other found objects
- Set up camp and cuddle in the tent right away
- Face your tent toward the rising sun
- Hang a hammock
- Stretch out in the grass or sand
- Set up a minibar
- Rig an outdoor shower
- Hang flags or tea lights from the branches
- Eat off fine china
- Kick off your shoes
- Light a fire immediately
- Move in!

Or, do what YOU want:
- Again: This space is yours for as long as you're here. Feel it. Own it. Make it yours.

3) Seek It: Check In With Your Surroundings

OK. You've checked into yourself and your home base. Now, it's time to orient and take in all that's around you.

So:
- What's the landscape? The seascape? The skyscape?
- Among your surroundings, what's new and alluring?
- What's curious and bizarre?
- What's beautiful and hideous?
- What's the local flavor?
- The local scene?
- What are the sounds, the smells, the textures?

Look around.
Take a minute to check in with your neighborhood. What's the vibe? Quaint? Bustling? Quiet? Junky? What's your first impression? Note it now and watch how it evolves through your vacation.

Map it out.
Find your nearest necessities. The breakfast joint, coffee shop, grocery store, wine shop, hot dog vendor. Jot down the places that you want to check out on your adventure.

Meet the locals.
Who are your neighbors? Who are your guides? Who has the dish? The concierge, the bartender, the sundry shop worker, the folks at the next campsite over? Ask around, open up, there are no stupid questions.

Check your hours.
When does the sun rise and set? How early does the diner open? How late does room service deliver? What are the hours of the pool? The exercise room? The spa? Timing is everything, right?

Move it.
Where's the nearest subway or bus or trolley stop? Is there a cabstand nearby? Bike or scooter rentals close to you? Where's the stuff to help you get around? Find it so you can hit it.

4) Live It: Check In With Your Hot Spots

Finally, to help you get grounded in your evolutionary Trip—and to center yourself on the what you'd like to learn from the universe as you're about to head out—refer back to those three Hot Spots you identified in the Prep section.

Quickly, flip back to your Life Map and take a look. What were your top three Life Areas? What emotions did you note about these Hot Spots? What did you want to change? And what were you grateful for? Take a moment to remember these Life Areas and bring them into the present moment.

Write down your 3 Hot Spots, along with 3 in-the-moment notions about each here or in your journal:

1.

2.

3.

Keep these top-of-mind as we move into the next experiment. **And we're off!**

[THE TRIP] Time for Your Morning Meds

*"We packed
whole lives into bundles in search
of what chooses us, what wants to come
back to the surface, what needs to be said.
We had so many dreams
we didn't know what to make of them."*

–Helene Cardona

Morning Meds? That's *meditations* for those in the know.

Fabulous. You're now ready to explore in a new way, to dive into your travels and make waves wherever you go. You're about to create awesome tsunamis of adventure all around.

And, every day, Morning Meds is a perfect place to start.

This experiment offers a space and time for morning or in-the-moment reflection and intention-setting during your journey. Designed to help you collect and record your thoughts while you're on vacation, it also offers some helpful tips for navigating throughout your day in a nimble, open and evolutionary way.

All to help you get the most out of your aliveness adventure on the road.

First thought: Homework doesn't exist on vacation, so do with these what you will. Hint: Try something today. And, naturally, you're free to do it differently tomorrow!

Next thought: This is your creation so make it count. Hint: You'll be glad you did once you head back home as Re-Entry has a lot of fun stuff that uses these insights.

And, here's how it works:

> **• Every morning, focus on the questions that give you the most energy**
> **• Use these ideas as a conduit to new learning**
> **• Jot down ideas and thoughts in your journal or directly in the book here**
> **• And always remember: your answers are within. Simple as that.**

Song of Myself:

First up, what do you know about yourself as you greet the day? And, most importantly, what do you want to do with that? Take a moment to ponder:

What are you feeling as you meet the sun or clouds or rain or snow?

What do you appreciate about what today offers you?

What are you thankful for before the day even begins?

My Perfect Day:

Next, ponder any and everything that would make today the best day ever: your dream day. Include experiences, encounters, activities, thoughts, nuances, notable adventures and more. Then, focus in on what gives you the most energy and ask yourself:

What intentions would I like to set for this dream day? Describe it here:

Today My Perspective Is:

What or who will you be today in order to bring your intentions to life? What kind of attention will you give your intentions?

What words and feelings define who you want to be today?

What energy will you give to your being and all you wish to create?

Baggage Check:

Hey! What's that showing up?! Yep, although you made a noble attempt, that dang baggage may have stowed away. Face it, confront it and choose what you want to do with it here!

Which stories are early risers and have shown up already?

Which baggage just won't seemingly go away?

And what will you do with this baggage now?

Hot Spot Visioning:

Next, while you're steeped in your defined intention and being for the day—and free from your baggage!—look again at your Hot Spots. How do they look viewed through this new baggage-free self? Through these new intentions? Through your Morning Meds as a whole? Ask yourself:

What do I want to learn about my Hot Spots today?

How will my purposeful being open up new possibilities for approaching my Hot Spots?

Make it Happen!

Finally, how will your being guide your doing in regard to your Hot Spots as well as the larger context of your adventures today?

What, within your perfect day and your purposeful being, will you do to lean in to the experience of this day?

What actions will bring your being and your intentions to life?

How do your Hot Spots look through the lens of these actions?

What do you hope to learn about your Hot Spots today?

NAV TIP: COME BACK TO YOU

As you savor a few, final minutes before you jump into your adventures, it's helpful to take a pause. Breathing is a super effective, super portable way to do this. We offered a breathing practice earlier and we have another for you to try before you launch your day. Here's how it goes:

1. Sit in a comfortable spot, close your eyes.

2. Take three deep breaths, all the way down to your belly, in through the nose and out through the mouth.

3. Then, slowly inhale through your nose. As you do, imagine that breath as a point of light. Starting at the base of your spine, breathe that point of light up your spine all the way out the top of your head.

4. As you exhale through your nose, imagine that point of light traveling back to the base of your spine in tandem with your breath.

5. Continue to slowly breathe that light up and down your spine.

Whether you do this for 3 minutes or 20, this practice is designed to bring your attention inward, will help you settle into your You-ness and bring a breath of fresh air to your world before you rock your day.

[THE TRIP] Trip Up Your Trip

"Somewhere, something incredible is waiting to happen."

–Carl Sagan

Your present point of power? Now.

Yowza. You've checked in with your room, your surroundings and yourself. You've played with Morning Meds and set some serious intentions. You've tapped into a new view of your Hot Spots. You've breathed in new possibilities of a centered and powerful You.

You're now ready to dive into that luscious, liminal space of adventure with the following in-the-moment experiments.

Meant to push you out of your comfort zone, these ideas offer ways to be the most alive you that you can imagine. They help you tap into your Hot Spots. They keep you on your toes, ready to seek and find all sorts of answers all hiding in plain sight.

So, kick that creature-of-habit habit to the curb and get ready for the oodles of new opportunities. The signs, the smells, the people, the experiences—all new things for you to try and do and learn—are right outside your door.

So, let's go. And live it up in the now.

Imagine: Theme Park

Time for some intentional fun! That is, to push your Trip a bit further and create a theme for your day! How about Regal? Crazy? Calm? Exploratory? Flirtatious? Sacred? Peaceful? Rock Star?

Decide your day's theme and carry it through the morning, afternoon, evening or entire vacation.

Ideas:

• Unpack your sense of humor: your hilarious, always-on, jokester side that keeps everyone rolling.
• Open up to some serenity: your calm, collected, centered side that floats through time and space.
• Prepare for VIP treatment: your best-dressed, super-swanky, hottie side that always gets the best table.
• Note: When the universe knows who it's dealing with, it has a much easier time catering the experience.

So, who is the universe dealing with? Jot down some thoughts here or in your journal:

Dare: Got the Guts?

Game time. Tear a sheet of paper into small pieces. Write down 20 dares—anything you can think of— and put the pieces of paper in an ice bucket or hat and pull a couple every morning or during the day. There. Instant adventure. Note: This is tons of fun with adventurous travel mates as well. Or strangers.

What do you dare to do on this trip? Put down some ideas here:

Ask: Language Lessons

What if you asked a perfect stranger for an opinion to your quandary? Or the cab driver for their recommendation or advice about your Hot Spots? Or your traveling companions what their purpose in life is? Or your family what their wildest hope for their future might be? What if you asked to be seated in the front row or at the best table or in the queen's or king's throne? If you never ask, you'll never know. Curiosity empowers, so open up to the questions and start inquiring! Hint: Being shy and playing small doesn't do anyone any good at all on your Trip. Especially you.

What questions do you have? Brainstorm:

Listen: Travel Guides

It's one thing to ask. It's another thing to listen. Most of the time, the majority of us are preparing our response while another is talking. Sound familiar? What about this instead: ask only to hear others' answers. Take in another person's ideas, seek out their messages, engage with your guides. What amazing gems of insight are waiting to be uncovered through a simple question and the ears to hear? Tip: On the Trip, make a commitment to interact with others differently. Starting now.

How can you listen differently? Who needs to be heard more?

Share: Inspire Others

What do you want to share with others about your Trip? Whether you choose to plant a haiku for a future—perhaps e>v!—traveler in the hotel info-binder or karaoke your favorite song at the top of your lungs or exist in a silent open-hearted space with the person next to you on the subway, what's in your beautiful being that connects with those around you? What's creative, inventive, inspirational, funny, quirky, thoughtful in you? Anywhere you can make your mark, make it! You have something to share!

What are some ways you can make your mark today?

See: Sign, Sign, Everywhere a Sign

The Trip isn't just about new territory. It can also be about old territory seen with new eyes. Or new territory seen with old eyes. So, open your eyes and notice. On the Trip, everything is a sign. Hint: Every. Single. Thing.

What do you see that speaks to you?

What's that billboard saying to you? That bumper sticker? That theatre marquee? That map? That graffiti?

What makes you laugh? What makes you run? Toward it? Away? What makes you cringe? Cry? Cackle?

Look to the ground: Pick up a rock. Or a feather. Always a penny. Keep it as a good luck charm. Make a wish. Believe it will come true.

What's your sign?

Reroute: Different is Good

What if you lived differently on your Trip and took a different route? What if you really spoke your truth to colleagues or friends or family? What if you tried something new from the menu or from a street vendor? What if you allowed yourself a different routine during the day: exercise or a reeeaally good meal or meditation? Or skipped those altogether? What if you gave yourself permission to go a little crazy? What if you did the souvenir thing differently and sent yourself a postcard? In other words, Different is all around, so invite her along. She's fun to travel with.

What's your *what if*?

What have you never tried that you could try today?

What new territory could you explore?

Recalibrate: What's the Gift?

No Tickets! No Seats! You Missed the Boat! Or did you?

What is the great gift in the seemingly bad thing that happened? What does this seemingly bad thing allow for? Could it actually have saved the day? Could it actually lead to something even more amazing?

Rise above frustrating situations and trust that there's something there. Open up. Be curious. Have a laugh. View your Hot Spots from 30,000 feet. Lots of different perspectives, lots of different options, lots of other words to use than bad or good. Ideas: intriguing, odd, quirky, hilarious, etc.

What are some other ways to describe frustrations on this Trip?

If something goes wrong today, what might be the hidden gift?

What can you do to stay present and in the flow with where the day takes you?

Play: The O'Mancy Family

Who? The O'Mancy Family!

Inspired by the original *Bibliomancy*—that fun practice of clearing your mind, posing a question for the type of insight you seek, opening a book randomly and placing your finger on the page: what's the text there? what answer does it tell you?—the O'Mancy Family was born.

Play with these ideas throughout your day. Ask a question, receive an answer. Explore your Hot Spots here. Have some fun with your travel partners. Get new friends you meet along the way involved. See what happens.

Bibliomancy:

Using the instructions above, play with your guide book, the magazine on your hotel desk, a novel you find in a café. The message or answer is there if you seek it. Close your eyes, think of a question, open the book and point. What does it tell you?

Artomancy:

Enter a gallery or museum, clear your thoughts, ask a question, close your eyes and have your travel partner lead you around, providing you with a right, left, forward or stop option at every crossroad, until you sense that you are in the place you want to be. Open your eyes. What do you see? What does it tell you? What is the impact on your senses? What is your answer or insight or a-ha?

Songomancy:

Clear your mind, set an intention or pose a question for the insight you seek and randomly select a song on your phone. What's the significance of the song? Where does it take you? If you have some time on a train or bus, put your player on shuffle and in between songs ask a quick question. The song will provide an often-amazing answer. Or: are you at a place with a TouchTunes or old-school jukebox? Ask a question and punch numbers at random. Then, listen.

GPS-omancy:

Before you venture out for the day, write down a sequence of directions: e.g. east, west, west, east, east. Walk it. See what you find. Or type in a random address into your phone or GPS. Explore.

Photo-omancy:

Open your photo gallery on your phone or on your friend's phone or a stranger's phone! Ask a question that needs some insight, close your eyes, scroll the gallery and point. What photo did you land on? What does it tell you?

You-Name-it-O'Mancy:

The O'Mancy family grows in direct proportion to your willingness to create it. Will it be nature-walk-omancy? Foreign phrase-book-omancy? Menu-omancy? Where will you set intentions and seek insights from your surroundings? Where will you allow your creativity to kick in?

Remember: Create a Mantra

Among all this repositioning and curiosity is one simple idea: it's not so much about being centered ALL the time but knowing your way back to center when you're not there. Mantras are a super-effective way to remember your way back to where you want to be.

Look around at the ideas that are resonating with you. Notice the signs and billboards and stickers and art and songs and conversations with your travel mates and new friends alike. Hold your penny for good luck. And now, create a short statement that really hits home. And use it.

To help you get back to center, to give you a boost, to simply have some fun, here are a few examples that have worked for others.

Take 'em, leave 'em, just get that motor runnin' to create your own!

Love and Abundance! / Be the hub. / Let go. / I belong. / I am courage. / Never hide. / Why not? / Where's the party? / YES! / Relaaaax.

Now, brainstorm a mantra of your own here or in your journal. Use it daily.

Celebrate: Toast Yourself

Finally, what's the deal with our tendency to be so gosh darn hard on ourselves? Our faults or trip-ups often receive a lot of our attention, while our strengths and triumphs are humbly brushed aside.

Not allowed on this Trip.

Celebrations can come in many different forms and, as long as they honor you, go for it! Some ideas:

- **Lead the café, restaurant or bar in an impromptu sing-along**
- **Jump in the fountain or pool or lake**
- **Buy yourself a gift—a really great one**
- **Buy a giant bundle of balloons and give them all to a soon-to-be-surprised kid**
- **Take a nap or get up late or really early just because you can**
- **Pop champagne just because it's Tuesday**
- **Dance, dance, dance. Just because!**
- **Add an extra day onto your vacation. An extra week. An extra month.**

Do something—anything!—to let yourself know that you appreciate the beautiful individual you are and the universe around you.

What are your most over-the-top ideas on how you will celebrate You on this trip?

Set the intention here. And make it happen.

[THE TRIP] Baggage Busters

"Here's my hunch: nobody's secure, and nobody feels like she completely belongs. Those insecurities are just job hazards of being human. But some people dance anyway, and those people have more fun."

–Glennon Doyle Melton

So, are you having fun? Rocking and rolling? Kicking ass? And taking names?

We bet you're exploring your vacation with a newfound energy.

We bet you're leaning into your experience with intention and attention.

And we bet you've started to catch a glimpse of that wonderful liminality and aliveness that this amazing world has to offer.

We also bet things are in flux and flexible, changing shapes and shifting quite often as well.

Yep, the Trip is often a back-and-forth of "Do I want to do this?" or "Do I want to do that?" and you may change your mind countless times.

The same goes for your intentions or priorities or goals.

In fact, finding yourself back at square one is often indicative that a real, tangible change is about to take place. And, sometimes, retreating to old behaviors is the biggest teacher of all.

It's a moment when you can stop, take a look around and say, "What's THAT about?!"

That's called noticing.

Awareness without judgment, noticing comes in very handy when old stories appear. Especially, those times when particularly persistent baggage shows up that you just can't shake.

You know, that super-heavy baggage that pops up and weighs you down? Like when you're tired or sad or quarrelling with your travel partner or insert-your-trigger-here? And you forget the best way to send it packing? And, instead, it sends you into a reactionary story-spiral that leaves you dizzy, disoriented and, maybe even, a bit sick to your stomach?

Well, remember this, Grasshopper:

You've packed every story into your baggage, so you're obviously capable of removing them as well.

That's right. You have complete control over what stays and what goes.

So, for tips, tricks and tasks on how to send your stories out of your life for good, read on.

You're about to learn some bona fide ways to crush those bad-boys once and for all.

You about to meet your Baggage Busters.

The Iceberg Approach: Dive Below the Surface

Try this on for size: Just as we can only see 10% of an iceberg's mass above the surface, there's a whole lot more going on with our baggage than meets the eye.

Or: We may think that whatever has triggered us is the cause of our irritation, dismay or sadness. Not so. What actually creates this reaction is a whole lot deeper.

Case in point: Author, psychologist and Buddhist-big-thinker Tara Brach says, "Suffering is our call to attention, our call to investigate the truth of our beliefs."

This is a game-changer because, suddenly, baggage is no longer an outside job. Instead, it's an inside job, through and through.

With this new reality, suffering doesn't happen to us. Instead, suffering might be because of us.

Now, be assured: this isn't about blame or shame. Instead, if we realize that suffering—read: baggage—is simply based on our beliefs about whatever has gotten under our skin, we're on a path to freedom.

Because we can do something about it.

So, let's go there.

Grounded in Cognitive Behavior Therapy and based on the work of psychologist Albert Ellis, let's play with a new equation that goes deeper than just the immediate, surface response you may have to baggage, suffering or external challenges.

Trigger + Story = After-Effect

Here's how it works:

1. First, pinpoint your Trigger:
    a. What set you off? Jot it down:
        • Was it something that actually occurred?
        • Something you anticipate occurring?
        • Something that's only occurred in your mind?

2. Next, note your Stories about the Trigger:
    a. What meaning are you making of this?
    b. Which of your rules, beliefs or expectations does it violate?

3. Third, identify the After-Effects:
    a. Based on your Stories about the Trigger, what are the consequences in your feelings and in your behaviors?
    b. What conclusions are you drawing? What future predictions are you making?
    c. Which of these stories, beliefs or demands are actually based in truth? Or based in your true, glorious essence? Be really really honest with yourself here. (Hint: It's likely very few.)

4. Now what? Adjust your lens and tell a new Story:
    a. In the spirit of G.K. Chesterton's quote—"An inconvenience is an adventure wrongly considered"—what if you adjusted your lens to be based on your truest intentions, your deepest core or the powerful, beautiful You inside?
    b. Tell the story of your Trigger from this vantage.
    c. Note how you now feel and what you will do.

And, voila. There's the whole iceberg. And, the whole of You, choosing not to suffer. **Dang, that's some enlightened mojo you got goin' on there.**

The Cape of Good Hope Approach: Make Peace With Your Baggage

Sometimes, the best way to release your baggage is to look past its outer fangs to get to its inner, positive intention. After all, your baggage must be serving you in some way or else you would have ditched it long ago, right?

Now, it's time to make peace and release.

First, to make peace with your baggage, search to see what it has been doing to help you.

For example, perhaps some stories you tell yourself keep you safe from, say, rejection. Another story might keep you from of acting irrationally. Perhaps a third protects you from doing something stupid.

The thing is, though:

> • These stories are layered with other stories. For example: What's so bad about rejection? What's so wrong with being irrational? Who hasn't done something stupid in their life?
> • And, then, THESE stories are made up of EVEN MORE stories: What do I actually believe about rejection? What do I really think about people who are irrational? What the heck does stupid mean anyway?
> • And on and on and on and on and on.

Once you see how deep your stories go, perhaps it's simply time to leave that baggage on the side of the road once and for all.

Give it peace, give it a release and, finito, you're free.

The Mount Everest Approach: You Don't Have to Climb This Sucker

Among and amidst your travels, you may notice that baggage often likes to show up in the form of strict certainty: Stories that place you steadfastly in an either/or challenge; stories that only take a black and white perspective; stories littered with words like always, never, should or ought to.

Heads up: this, friend, is baggage of gigantic, mountainous proportions.

Instead, when a reaction like this appears, take a breath (or 10) and ask yourself if any of what you're experiencing is actually true. Or: While strict certainty is one perspective you could take, there are 1,000,000 others out there that could serve you better and be more accurate.

Ask yourself:

Which perspective do you want to take as you encounter a frustrating person or situation? Then, once you've opened up to new possibilities, choose a perspective that best serves the real You like:

- **What's this view from a hot air balloon? From a plane? From the space station?**
- **Will this matter one year from now?**
- **What's a child's perspective?**
- **What would your hero, totem animal or inner elder say about this situation?**
- **What if this challenge were a gift?**

The only thing that's certain? You're the Editor-in-Chief, remember? When you notice stories that don't serve you, call for a rewrite! And take a different slant, view or perspective. **Pronto.**

The GPS Approach: Reposition Yourself

Hit a super snag? Feeling completely stuck? Can't get over it? **At all?**

As we've discussed, manifestation is brought to life through the attention we give our intentions.

If, however, what you're experiencing throughout the day is not matching up to the mood or vibe you crave, you can usually bet there's been a derailment along the Be, Do, Know continuum. And your baggage is right there to remind you of the crash.

No problem.

This is the perfect opportunity to check and correct.

Notice when your stories show up that whatever you're feeling on the inside will usually act as a mirror to what you're experiencing (read: creating) around you. For example, ponder the feelings (being) and actions (doing) related with each of these statements:

> **"I am annoyed and impatient with this situation."**
> **vs.**
> **"I am a flexible being, going with the flow."**

What do you think will be manifested with each? If you're giving attention to stories of feeling annoyed and impatient? Yep, probably more annoyance and impatience.

Instead, if you're focused on a new perspective such as remaining flexible and nimble, what do you think you'll get? Yep, you got it. More flexible and nimble. News flash: **sometimes it's really that easy.**

The Mount Olympus Approach: Unleash Your Inner God/dess

Finally, it's time to face the ultimate baggage of gigantic proportions: the stories that play arch nemesis to your inner hero.

You know, the inner You who is fabulously strutting around, living it up until one little stumble over a pebble of insecurity conjures up the evil enemy—your baggage—sending you tumbling down a slippery slope of stories?

At these moments, it's time to bring in the big guns: your super powers.

> **• So, what are your powers?**
> **• What is it about you that dazzles and delights, inspires and amazes?**
> **• What makes you feel proud, jazzed, hopped up, energized?**
> **• Who is your inner hero?**
> **• What does he or she look like? Sound like? Walk like? Talk like?**

Seriously. Stop a moment. Close your eyes and summon the image of you as that being: A gorgeous, all-powerful, freakin' god/dess. See that image clearly in your mind and notice your energy shifting to that place of breathtaking strength.

Feel it, see it and lock in that energy.

That is You. When your evil nemesis comes lurking around, call on that image, feel that energy and ask what your god/dess would do right then and there.

And: KAPOW! Onward.

The Great Wall Approach: Find Your Protective Barrier

Here's an easy one: If you find your baggage weighing you down, stop and make a quick list of very nice yet very simple things about yourself—things that are so basic they'll make you giggle. Ideas: "I like my hair." Or: "My cat loves me." Or: "I have a keen sense of humor."

Now, when your baggage shows up and tries to weigh you down, stop what you are doing, take out your list, pick a phrase and say it in your head:

> **"I like my hair."**
> **"I like my hair."**
> **"I like my hair."**

Why?

In this case, the simple, goofy or silly phrase is not about affirmation or positive reinforcement.

Instead, this phrase is simply here to STOP your story in its tracks. To put up a (great) wall between your baggage and you.

You see, our brains give energy to streams of thought —remember: where the attention goes, the energy flows. So this phrase is a simple, basic, neutral thought that STOPS a non-helpful thought in action.

In short, no need to give energy to stories that keep you where you were.

This phrase acts as a reset button to get your thoughts back on track, willing and able to focus on where you want to go and what you want to create. **Now.**

The Napa Approach: Would You Like Some Cheese With that W(h)ine?

Soooo, you're steeping in baggage and, frankly, not interested in taking—or even finding—the freakin' high road right now. Instead, you'd prefer to cry in your beer or pinot or sodie pop, thank you very much. Or have a hissy fit. Or throw down your stupid phone. Or roll your eyes at your annoying travel partner. Or, or, or.

Fine. Go with it. Indulge it. Feel it. Express it.

But don't stop at plain old melancholy. Really throw yourself into the scene. Like 3-year-old temper-tantrum. In the supermarket. On the floor. At the top of your lungs.

Yep, take a deeeeep breath and in the whiniest, most poor-me voice you can muster, let 'er rip. And repeat exactly what your baggage is telling you:

- "But I wanted that museum to be open today!!! Things never work out for meeeeeee!"
- "I hate what jet-lag does to my skin!! I look terrrrrrible!"
- "You're not paying attention to meeeee! I should just be here by myseeeelf!"
- "This weather SUUUUCKS!! I can't believe I'm wasting my vacation time here!!!"

Wait a minute. What's that? A smile? A chuckle?

Welcome back, You. Sometimes the best antidote for your baggage is to play out its message in the biggest, most dramatic way possible and then giggle at how goofy it sounds. Once again, you've broken the spell and returned to choice. **You rock.**

NAV TIP: SET IT & FORGET IT

Holy. Cow.

Great job facing your baggage head on. You're really getting into this Trip and people are starting to notice.

A final tip to remember? Stay present in your learning. And don't forget to enjoy the journey.

This vacation, this adventure is here to help you break out of your mold, to help you unearth new possibilities.

And, most of all, to help you have even more fun along the way.

If things are getting heavy, or if you're feeling too much pressure, take a break. Take a breather. Pull back a while.

Conversely, if you're enjoying the intensity, surprises and a-ha moments that the games, questions and experiments are bringing up, dive in deeper. Move in closer. Explore even more.

All in all, this is your Trip.

Live it and experience it your way.

Every single day.

[THE TRIP] Evening Impressions

"The most beautiful thing we can experience is the mysterious."

–Albert Einstein

Good night, you daring adventurer.

What a day. What a whirlwind. What an exploration. Your adventure has, no doubt, been packed.

To recap: You've set awesome intentions. You've played with ideas, experiences and learning. You've stood toe to toe with your baggage. You've seen your Hot Spots engage with the world. And you've challenged yourself in exciting ways.

All in all, it's been a jam-packed experience full of the new. And the old. And, sometimes, the new in an old way and the old in a new way!

So, what's made an impression on you? What have you done to create this experience? What do you want more or less of? What worked and what felt taxing?

Take a moment to capture the cool stuff, the challenging bits, the things that still don't make sense. Ask your travel mates to play along or sneak off by yourself. Gather it all to see what answers tomorrow brings. Or the next day. Or the next. And remember, it's all about the journey. All. The. Time.

What I Loved About Today:

What were the highlights? Especially those unexpected conundrums that just happened to turn out beautifully? What did you learn? How has today been good to and for you? What made today, well, today?

Jot down your thoughts here or in your journal. (Including how & where your Hot Spots appeared!)

Today's Surprises:

What did you notice or tune into—street signs, billboards, people, conversations—that turned your head? What was the impact? What made you smile? **What surprised you today?**

Today's Challenges:

What was outside of your comfort zone? What did you choose to Be, Do or Know that you never thought you would or could? What pushed you? How did you deal with it? **What challenged you today?**

What I Didn't Get About Today:

What left you with questions? What left you with your brow creased and your tongue tied? Where did your baggage appear? **What queries did today bring?**

Tonight As I Drift Off:

What are the thoughts or feelings you will take into your sleepy time? What answers can a good night's rest bring? What insights do you seek? **Write down a question to be answered in your dreams.**

[THE TRIP] Final Trip Talk

"All you need is the plan, the road map, and the courage to press on to your destination."

–Earl Nightingale

Fantastic.

You're on the Trip of a lifetime.

You're moving and shaking.

You're exploring and expanding.

Now, as you get ready to do it all over again tomorrow, check out a few final reminders to keep you light on your feet and focused on aliveness through the rest of your Trip.

> • **Remember to live in liminality:** Your vacation is the perfect space of betwixt and between. This is the time of pure possibility. Be aware, it's around you as we speak.

> • **Review your Morning Meds for patterns or new possibilities of being:** Asking for the same perfect day that doesn't seem to appear? Try a new perspective. Seeing the same baggage pop up again and again? Time for a Be tweak.

> • **Feeling not-so-hot about your Hot Spots?** Take another look at your Life Map. Anything else stand out or feel more important now that you're on the road? Change it up.

• **You've already checked in? You sure?** No one says you can't rearrange your room or camp mid-journey. Check in along the way: move stuff around, try the OTHER breakfast joint tomorrow, take the bus instead of the train, walk instead of cab.

• **Take a breath!** Inhale, exhale, repeat. Open up to new energy.

• **Trip up your Trip constantly:** Try a new adventure a day, a new theme, a mantra, the O'Mancy family. Have some goofy, giddy, all-out-there fun. This is vacation, remember?

• **No excuses allowed:** Be ultra-intentional about kicking your stories to the curb. They didn't pay to take this vacation with you. No freeloaders, man.

• **Recap it:** Evening Impressions are a great way to wind down and take stock at the end of the day as well as a sweet chance to infuse your dreamtime with incredible intentions. Dig deep, get it out there, trust it all and allow the universe to offer some answers.

• **Finally:** Every day on your vacation, put your bookmark back to the beginning of this section and see how these experiments—and you!—change.

See you tomorrow!

[RE-ENTRY]

[RE-ENTRY] Welcome Back

"Be daring, be different, be impractical, be anything that will assert integrity of purpose and imaginative vision against the play-it-safers, the creatures of the commonplace, the slaves of the ordinary."

–Cecil Beaton

Welcome home! You have stepped into your aliveness and what a journey it has been.

It's fabulous: you've learned how to create your reality. It's exciting: you've intentionally stretched yourself in new ways. It's inspiring: you've witnessed light-bulb moments about yourself. And you're ready for more!

Just in time, Re-Entry is here.

• As Prep helped you tap into your Being...

• And the Trip allowed your Being to guide your Doing...

• Re-Entry—and all its dimensions—is Knowing what this journey has revealed to you now that you're home again. And deciding where you'd like to go next.

So, let's hit it.

NAV TIP: THINK GLOBALLY, EVOLVE LOCALLY

Reminder time! The main reason for the entire *Evolution Through Vacation* movement?

To create a life where every day feels like a vacation day.

This is where Re-Entry comes in.

Not only will this section help you make even more sense of the excitement you've just had on the Trip, it'll also equip you with tools and techniques to keep this vacation energy alive through your everyday journeys moving forward.

As Cecil's quote says:

"To push against the commonplace. To elevate beyond the play-it-safers."

As e>v says:

To live a life that's truly alive. No matter where you are.

So, buckle up.

The ride ain't over yet.

[RE-ENTRY] Landing Gear

"There is nothing like returning to a place that remains unchanged to find the ways in which you yourself have altered."

–Nelson Mandela

Comin' in hot.

You notice it. Others notice it, too. Something about you is different. Whatever that is—perspectives, relationships, outlooks, options—you have changed.

That can be exciting. And scary. All at the same time.

> **• You may have returned from your trip with a heightened sense of self that you can't wait to share, and your landing will be easy and full of joy. How brilliant and empowering that is.**

> **• You may have returned from your adventure with new realizations that are not so comfortable. This awareness is also a gift; sometimes the most turbulent landings cause you to appreciate that you've simply arrived.**

> **• You may have returned steeped in your magic spell of Be, Do, Know, ready to live that way forever more. Or not.**

No matter what, as you get resettled in your life, the first step is to get clear on what shifted while you were away. Let's get the wheels spinning.

• First up, take a look back at your Life Map and Hot Spots.
• Read through your Morning Meds and Evening Impressions.
• Dive into any other jottings, scribbles or doodles you created and ask yourself:

• What's new?

• What's not?

• What's valuable?

• What's changed?

• What's different?

Jot down your initial thoughts. Then take a look at the categories ahead, ponder your journey and get it all down in one, handy-dandy spot to track your Re-Entry. **And your evolution!**

Hot Spots:

In more depth, take a look at the Hot Spots that you focused on throughout your journey: flip back through your notes and revisit your first impressions. In light of all you've been through, it can be fun and illuminating to see your initial jottings. Even more, the shifts are often quite striking when pre- and post-thoughts are juxtaposed.

My Three Hot Spots were, are or changed to:

What I noticed about my Hot Spots before my journey:

What I notice about my Hot Spots now:

Souvenirs:

Next, while the term *souvenir* might call to mind t-shirts, shot glasses or other trinkets, the word itself is actually French for *memory*. So, let's talk souvenirs; let's talk memories. What's important for you to remember from this vacation?

Highlights:
What do you recall about how you held yourself, how you interacted with others that was really alive? What were your Hot Spot highlights and gleaming moments? **Jot down thoughts:**

A-Ha Moments:
What was refreshing? In what ways did you surprise yourself or allow others or the Universe to surprise you? **Any Hot Spot a-ha moments?**

Gifts:
What are you super grateful for as you return? What are new insights and perspectives that you picked up along the way? **In your Hot Spot areas and beyond?**

Baggage:

You bravely checked your stories and created a new packing list. So, what baggage stayed at home and what did you carry along? What did you, perhaps, discover hiding? What did you ditch mid-trip?

Stories:
Which stories showed up that you thought you'd left behind? Or didn't even realize you had packed until you arrived? **List a few here:**

Challenges:
What was difficult? What pushed you or your Hot Spots to the limit? **Be honest, no censoring:**

Surprises:
What shocked you about your baggage? **What bewildered you?**

Freedom:
What baggage did you consciously release? **How did it feel?**

Declarations:

Finally, did you have THAT moment?

When something so amazing happened that you vowed to change a part of your life to keep it alive?

Or, when you met someone who inspired you and, now that you're home, you can't wait to bring a new kind of energy to your existence?

Or, you had such a lovely time doing XYZ—something that gave a new perspective on your Hot Spots or life —that you've planned to keep it around every day?

Declare it here. Make it real. And make it count.

What one thing will you commit to right now that will amp up your aliveness?

Ponder a while.

Then, WRITE IT BIG. Right here:

[RE-ENTRY] Liminal Living

"Remember, life can be found only in the present moment. The past is gone, the future is not yet here, and if we do not go back to ourselves in the present moment, we cannot be in touch with life."

–Thich Nhat Hanh

Nice!

You've recapped your journey and your Hot Spots. You've played with highlights and a-ha moments. You've really started to tap into this aliveness business with a bona fide declaration of action.

Now, let's bring it back to the core idea that started this whole thing: liminality.

You remember liminality, right? That expansive, freeing, open, malleable space of betwixt and between that you found on vacation?

And, you remember the secret about liminality, right? That, when living in the present moment—or *the now*—all space and time becomes liminal? And when you commit to living in the now, your entire existence can be a perpetual trip? An ongoing journey? A continual voyage? A beautiful, albeit temporary, pit stop between—sit down here— your birth and death?

Yep: Your entire life is a vacation when you live in the present moment. In this liminal space and time surrounding you right now.

Not the future (all speculation). Not the past (over and done). The present is where it's at. The present is where you're at.

The present is pure liminality.

It's the only time when anything and everything can happen in your life. It's the only moment you truly have control over. It's the only space where complete and utter possibility exists. And your recent adventure—being on vacation—gave you a glimpse into this. Into what the rest of your life can feel like every single day. And you're ready for it.

Liminal Living: The Idea

Liminal living, and Re-Entry as a whole, is the idea that you are free to create every day of your life in any way you like, just like you did on vacation.

Every day can be filled with exploration and curiosity and wonder, just like it was on vacation.

Every day provides the opportunity for choice and options and going with the flow, just like you experienced on vacation.

Every day, you decide how to move through life, how to act, how to respond, how to treat others and, most importantly, how to treat yourself.

Just. Like. On. Vacation.

Often, people come to these types of realizations only after tragedy or trauma.

A heart attack finally wakes us up to the fact that each day is a gift. A sudden loss motivates us to quit that soul-sucking job and finally go after our dreams. Or to open up to love. Or to get healthy. Or to simply live each day to the fullest.

Waking up can also happen with liminal living, with being present, with experiencing the now.

Even better: this is what your recent vacation revealed to you.

And even more: This is the pure possibility now available to you.

Anywhere. Anytime.

No tragedy necessary.

Liminal Living: The Practice

But, how do you do it?

Yes, we know. It's one thing to spew hippy-dippy, coffee-mug, kitten-poster mantras. It's another to really live it when daily stress reappears, when responsibility rushes back in, when the day-to-day cramps your style.

The good news?

The method is surprisingly straightforward, but the impact is big. You simply practice and repeat what you just did on the road.

In the Intro, you engaged with ideas of aliveness:
- **Liminality Is Everywhere**
- **You Write Your Story**
- **Life is a Rite of Passage**

Then, in Prep, you embodied the e>v magic spell of:
- **Be: The energy you give**
- **Do: The action you take**
- **Know: The insight you gain**

On your Trip, you embraced liminality by:
- **Checking In**
- **Busting Your Baggage**
- **Exploring Your Hot Spots**

And, just in time for the daily practice of liminal living—of truly making every day feel like a vacation day—you'll now keep it alive through:
- **Courage**
- **Possibility**
- **Choice**

Throughout your journey, you harnessed the power of big-thinking concepts that helped you create a tangible space and sense of aliveness.

Now, as you read on, play with the following experiments and insights in that same spirit and sense of wonder.

And get ready for the amazing life that's patiently waiting for you.

[RE-ENTRY] Courage First

"Courage is not the absence of fear, but rather the judgment that something else is more important than fear."

–Ambrose Redmoon

First and foremost, living every day like a vacation day starts with courage.

Courage is the first step toward recognizing liminality and confronting any road-blocks.

Courage allows you to be in the moment without knowing what the future will bring.

Courage calls forth your bold heart to embody all of you, whatever comes your way.

Courage is a being word, idea, concept and space of the utmost engagement, through-and-through.

Courage is what frees you to shift into possibility and, ultimately, into doing what serves you best.

In short, courage allows movement.

To move through life, it takes courage to bravely face your external world.

To move into your aliveness, it takes courage to bravely face your internal world.

Yep, to move our dreams forward, to make them a reality, we must have the courage to look inside, to take responsibility for ourselves, to be accountable to our emotions and, as James Hollis says in his incredible book, *Swamplands of the Soul*, to fully face "the nature of our nature."

Or: before you can shift into authentic movement toward your aliveness, and before you can truly attain all the wonderful things waiting for you in this life, it takes the courage to stop and examine any tendencies that might be holding you back from reaching these very objectives.

Also known as your hidden resistances.

Your unknown barriers.

Your self-sabotage.

As you journeyed through e>v, you met some of these challenges head-on when you faced your baggage.

You stood up to outdated or outmoded thinking that wasn't serving you.

You tackled and even stopped certain baggage from accompanying you on your recent vacation.

You bravely addressed the stories you were consciously aware of.

Now, to bring this into your everyday life and to achieve real, in-the-moment aliveness and liminal living, it's time to go even deeper.

It's time to seek out your unconscious self.

It's time to get to know what psychologist Carl Jung called, your "Shadow self."

Shadow Basics: Expand Your Consciousness to Expand Your Courage

As you're probably aware, your internal self or being consists of two levels:

The *Conscious* and the *Unconscious*.

> 1. The self you show to the external world, often based on external, cultural learning, is known as your Ego; it is the **conscious** sense you have about who you are.

> 2. Your Shadow, on the other hand, is your **unconscious** self; the internal being you might be unaware of or, even, hiding from the external world out of shame or fear.

To understand the relationship between Ego and Shadow, consider this:

You may express or exhibit certain personality traits based on outside approval or expectation, for better or worse.

Simultaneously, you may also have certain tendencies that you've rejected—that still exist internally—because of this same external expectation. Again, for better or worse!

For example:

When you were a child, maybe you learned it was unattractive for girls to display anger or that it was shameful for boys to show weakness. These past learnings influence how you now act (or don't) in the external world through your Ego.

But the tricky part is:

Whether you display these traits or not—in this example, anger or weakness—they still, and will always, exist within you as your Shadow.

These aspects of your personality are a part of you, even if they're rejected or denied.

Or: even though you may have stuffed down anger or weakness those feelings haven't gone away. Instead, that anger or weakness is constantly trying to escape from an internal prison via your Shadow, sometimes bursting at the seams to be included in your psyche. (You've seen it before: super-sweet girl with the zero-to-60 temper. Overly-macho boy with the soft underbelly he desperately tries to hide.)

And, the irony?

As Jungian psychology attests, the more you deny these rejected traits, the more the undercurrent swirls and the more these tendencies—this Shadow— unwittingly appears and acts out in often sneaky, counterproductive or self-sabotaging ways. And, sometimes, at the most inopportune times. With the most undesirable outcomes.

So, what do you do? You find the courage to face it.

"Wait, wait, wait! According to Jung, my Shadow is the person I'd rather not be! The parts of my personality that I'm ashamed of and embarrassed by! So, why in the world would I want to unearth these negative traits? This scary side? Why would I want to face old pains, ancient hurts or stuff that I've been successfully ignoring for many years, thank-you-very-much?"

Simple:

Because, the bottom line is this: This aspect of yourself—your Shadow—is present in your day-to-day life whether you are aware of it or not.

And your Shadow is often blatantly apparent to others, whether you know it or not.

And, quite frankly, your Shadow could be seriously mucking up your path to your goals and your ambitions and your freakin' dream life.

Whether. You'd. Like. To. Admit. It. Or. Not.

So, what's the remedy?

All together now: **Courage.**

According to Jung, and soon to be taken to the next step by you, if you have the courage to face your Shadow and, even more, if you have the courage to integrate your Shadow into your being, you have the possibility to reach personal wholeness and completeness.

You have the possibility to be free of the rusty chains that keep you from manifesting whatever your heart desires.

You have the possibility to, well, find new possibilities to bring your dream life to life.

Case in point:

Author Jacob Nordby says, "Every pain, addiction, anguish, longing, depression, anger or fear is an orphaned part of us seeking joy, some disowned shadow wanting to return to the light and home of ourselves."

Or: your pain, addiction, anguish, longing, depression, anger or fear is your Shadow. In the flesh. A bona fide entity. The real deal.

And your courage is about to give it some light.

By unearthing the courage to admit that you are the very things you'd rather not be, by having the courage to look at your own judgments of those very tendencies, and, most of all, by finding the courage to stop projecting judgment onto others, you are free.

Free to make new choices. Free to live liminally. Free to become alive.

Courage in Action:

Let's start to bring this to life. Take a moment to journal answers to these questions. Be open and honest with yourself. Bring your courage to the surface. And face your Shadow. You can do it.

First up, which parts of your personality are your favorite(s)? Which get accolades from the outside world? (Your kindness? Generosity? Sense of humor?) List traits you possess and display that get positive feedback from your friends and family:

How does this positive feedback make you feel? (Proud? Fulfilled? Whole?) Do you feel the same level of positivity toward yourself, inwardly?

On the flip side, which of your personality traits embarrass you? Or feel shameful? (Your temper? Anger? Or, conversely, showing vulnerability or sensitivity?) This is your Shadow self; list traits of your Shadow self here:

How do you feel when your Shadow self appears? (Bad? Upset? Guilty? Do you berate yourself? Judge yourself?) Journal for a while without censorship about how your Shadow self makes you feel:

Now take a deep breath. What might happen if you brought a sense of courage to your Shadow instead? What if you spoke with your Shadow face-to-face, bravely and honestly?

Example: if you're ashamed of appearing needy, or embarrassed by showing a side of you that desires support or help, could you sit with that feeling of neediness and examine why you might feel that way?

Could you bravely just be with your neediness and allow it to show you why it wants to hide away? Could you unearth a moment when, perhaps as a child, you were told to "buck up" or "figure it out" or "stop crying" or "I don't have time to help you, why can't you be more confident like other kids?" A time when you were told that neediness was considered bad or wrong?

Could you talk to the child within yourself and tell him or her that it's OK now? That you will help them? That you have time for them? That you will support them?

What does your inner child want to hear from you? Jot down thoughts here...

What does this courage do to your Shadow self? What does it feel like and look like to you now? Is there a space opening up for forgiveness? Journal a bit on this topic…

NAV TIP: FINAL SHADOW THOUGHTS

Psychologist Carl Jung explained the Shadow in this way:

"As children we learn to 'lock away' parts of ourselves that we judge (and are told) are wrong or inappropriate … this shadow exerts a powerful negative effect if left unacknowledged and unincorporated into our full being. Ironically, the more actively we deny and repress shadow content, the more it colors how we experience and show up in the world."

Instead of pushing your Shadow away, what if you embraced it? What if your Shadow became a re-integrated part of your being?

How might that feel?

[RE-ENTRY] Possibility Play

"Life is not a problem to be solved but an experiment to be lived."

–James Hollis

Just like the best adventures, we're starting to see that anything is possible.

You've bravely checked out your Shadow. You've eyed it, poked around it, jabbed at it. Maybe even tried to befriend it.

For some, this may have been engaging and enlightening. And, for others, your Shadow might still feel a little scary. Yucky. Even, not true.

And that's OK.

Re-Entry is a process. The courage to go to the dark places is step one. Now, step two is the possibility that you can re-imagine yourself; you can live in the present; you can create something new.

Or, as we just discussed, the majority of us follow rules we learned when we were small: "This is good, this is bad, this is acceptable, this is not." These guidelines have shaped our lives; these accolades and/or criticisms have created our Shadow. And again, in light of possibility: this is OK.

Why?

Because, possibility isn't about creating defense mechanisms against your Shadow. Possibility is about finding new uses and meaning *for* your Shadow.

Possibility is about making yourself available to the unexpected nuggets of unlimited options around you all the time. It's freedom, liberation, release, re-working. It's what you're ready for when you're ready for anything. It's re-writing your life script with a more expansive narrative. (Let's say it one last time: You are, after all, the Editor-In-Chief!)

So, let's play with Possibility.

Author and Ayurvedic physician Vasant Lad says, "Within every drop is the ocean and within every cell is the intelligence of the whole body."

So, how about a new way to look at the inherent intelligence that exists within you right this very moment? An exercise to uncover insights bubbling below the surface? An experiment that might look familiar, but completely new, in the most refreshing way?

You got it.

Here's a twist on the original Life Map but, this time around, it takes some new turns. It asks you to really trust the process. To go with the flow. To let things unfold.

All to help you tap into your inner being.

All to help you integrate the light and the dark.

All to bring you one step closer to living each day in the most alive way possible.

1) Color Your World

First, grab some markers, crayons or colored pencils and, on the Life Map below, color each of the continents with one of these shades: Red, Orange, Yellow, Green, Blue, Indigo, Violet

Once again, there are seven continents and seven colors. Pair 'em up. For any reason you want. Simple as that. (If you're not into coloring, just write a color on each continent or make a list in your journal and assign a color to each, you dig?)

Example:

Maybe it's a weather connection: yellow = sunny = Africa. Could be an energy you give to a color: blue = cold = Antarctica. Could be another association entirely: green = Ireland = Europe. Don't think too hard about it, just assign a color to each.

2) Feel Your World

OK. Have each of the continents paired with a color? Great. Now, either on the map or in your journal, write down three things that excite you about each continent and/or color and three words that ... don't.

Example:

Does yellow mean *vibrant, fun, happy* as well as *danger* or *caution* or *too bright?!* Does North America make you think of *freedom* and *diversity* as well as *divide*d or *materialistic*? How would it make you feel to go to one of the continents you've never visited? *Excited*, *giddy* and *adventurous* as well as *scared*, *timid* and *nervous*?

Go with your first thoughts and impressions and jot down your words on the Life Map or in your journal.

3) Rate Your World

One last step: Look at the continents again and, in the circle on the Life Map or in your journal, assign each continent a number from 1-7.

Again, don't think too hard about it. Simply go with your gut and rate the continents based on a scale of one (1) being the continent/color/words where you feel the *most* energy and seven (7) being the continent/color/words where you feel the *least* energy.

Remember:

Your first thought is your best thought. So just put a number by each. 1-7. Easy peasy.

Done! (Wait, what did you do?)

Congrats.

You just tapped into a different way to access wisdom about yourself and completed a Life Map without necessarily knowing it.

Or:

By living in the now, by trusting the process of the exercise, by capturing random thoughts, words and colors, you were unconsciously mining valuable ideas and concepts from your inner being.

And:

By bringing this internal self to the surface, you might have revealed some things you may not have been fully aware of. You might have opened up new possibilities by letting go of control. You might have just gotten a peek into your Shadow.

Here's how:

As you know, in addition to assigning words and numbers to the seven continents, this new Life Map incorporated seven colors.

Why?

Because these are the seven colors that align with the seven chakras in the human body which—get this— also map to the seven Life Areas.

Cool.

But, hold on. What's a *chakra?*

Chakra is Sanskrit for *circle* or *wheel.*

According to many spiritual traditions—Hindu and Tantric Buddhism in particular—humans have seven chakras, each representing an energy center within the body.

Chakras have been shown to physically correspond with our nerve centers and endocrine system; they've also been correlated with particular attributes and represent the intersection of mind, body and spirit in these areas.

To illustrate: the heart chakra exists, you guessed it, near your heart and relates to love and connectedness with others.

To maintain wellness, the chakras must be open and the energy flowing. If a chakra is blocked, energy doesn't flow easily and an imbalance appears. This may show up as a mental, emotional or physical ailment in your life.

Another tip?

Chakras are also associated with the good ol' ROY-G-BIV color spectrum. Cool. And easy to remember.

Which brings us back to this Life Map v2 experiment.

First, let's look at a brief description of each chakra and how it aligns with each Life Area.

NOTE: The info ahead was inspired by Vicki Howie's *Chakra Chart.* Also, there's lots more articles, books and guides out there on chakras if you want to explore this topic further.

RED • Root • Health • To Be

Physical existence. Survival and strength. Security. Stability. Healthy life structure, including finances and career. **Element:** Earth / **Sense:** Smell / **Basic Need:** Safety

ORANGE • Sacral • Stuff • To Feel

The senses. Creativity. Enjoyment. Aesthetics. Desire. Art and nature. Sexual energy. Adaptability. **Element:** Water / **Sense:** Taste / **Need:** Variety

YELLOW • Solar Plexus • Play • To Act

Energy. Vitality. Charisma. Humor. Achieving. Winning. Self-confidence. Personal power. Sense of identity. **Element:** Fire / **Sense:** Sight / **Need:** Significance

GREEN • Heart • Relationships • To Love

Emotional belonging. Intimacy. Love for self and others. Sharing. Acceptance. Hope. Trust. Compassion. Forgiveness. **Element:** Air / **Sense:** Touch / **Need:** To Love & Be Loved

BLUE • Throat • Expression • To Express

Authentic self-expression. Communication. Voicing. Listening. Influencing. Speaking one's truth. Virtue. **Element:** Sound / **Sense:** Hearing / **Need:** To Express Truth

INDIGO • Third Eye • Purpose • To Perceive

Vision. Dreams. Insight. Intuition. Intellectual exploration. Learning. Knowledge. Mental organization. Clarity. **Element:** Light / **Sense:** Intuition / **Need:** To Perceive

VIOLET • Crown • Spirit • To Know

Unity. Wisdom. Miracles. Bliss. Self-knowing. Being one. Inspiration. Enlightenment. **Element:** Consciousness / **Sense:** None / **Need:** To Know

Got it? Great.

Now, bet you know what's next. Yep, let's see where your colors, words and numbers landed! To get started, put all your info into a convenient list, either here in the book or in your journal.

RED • Root • Health • To Be
Continent:
Positive words:
Critical words:
Ranking:
Notes:

ORANGE • Sacral • Stuff • To Feel
Continent:
Positive words:
Critical words:
Ranking:
Notes:

YELLOW • Solar Plexus • Play • To Act
Continent:
Positive words:
Critical words:
Ranking:
Notes:

GREEN • Heart • Relationships • To Love
Continent:
Positive words:
Critical words:
Ranking:
Notes:

BLUE • Throat • Expression • To Express
Continent:
Positive words:
Critical words:
Ranking:
Notes:

INDIGO • Third Eye • Purpose • To Perceive
Continent:
Positive words:
Critical words:
Ranking:
Notes:

VIOLET • Crown • Spirit • To Know
Continent:
Positive words:
Critical words:
Ranking:
Notes:

Done? Let's find some learning.

Equipped with your recently-filled-out chart, take a look at it as a whole. Review the Life Area descriptions in line with your colors, your adjectives and your ratings. Sit with it a minute, notice connections, habits and learnings. Then answer:

Overall, what ideas, insights or possibilities are coming up for you that you may not have been aware of? What's there?

What are your three positive and three critical words telling you about the Life Areas? About your Ego? Your Shadow? Anything make you bristle? Anything drop your jaw? Anything appear that might resemble unconscious thoughts? How you positively or critically view aspects of yourself? Courageously explore what amazes, what feels right-on and what's puzzling. Face your brightest light and your darkest Shadow:

What do the numbers add to the big picture? Are there new Hot Spots here? Things that want your—or your Shadow's—attention? Explore them here:

Next, what about your body? Note where your colors or continents line up with the chakras. Any learnings that get a big reaction? A big *no*!? Or a big *yes*!? Jot down thoughts (see the pic for reference):

Finally, consider this: This new Life Map experiment is a great way to tap into what's going on beneath the surface. Sometimes our brains overwhelm our other wisdom-gathering apparatus. This experiment is a cool way to outsmart ourselves and learn something in the process. So, sit with your learnings a while. Play with the possibilities. Even, put it on the shelf and let the learning come later.

Hint: The learning always comes.

[RE-ENTRY] The Choice is Yours

"Life is a mirror and will reflect back to the thinker what he thinks into it."

–Ernest Holmes

Finally, what do you choose to create?

You've stepped fully into Re-Entry and liminal living. You've courageously begun to understand your Shadow and its effect on your life. You've learned more about who you are and how you can begin to live in the space of possibility.

Now, it's time for the ultimate question: what are you going to do about it? What will you choose?

Find out in a Vision Quest.

In order for you to manifest what you want in your life, it's important to have a clear picture of what that is; an image of what you choose. A Vision Quest is the perfect experiment to do so.

It's where you take your recently re-discovered courage and possibilities and create a vision—your choice—of the most amazing things your life could be or offer. It's where you leave your roadblocks behind and move into brave action. It's where you re-imagine your full potential and reach for the stars. It's where your personal growth and learning propel you into a vision for the future. Your future.

So, what's it gonna be?

Just like planning and envisioning your vacation, now it's time to do the same with your entire life. Start imagining. Start dreaming. Start visualizing exactly what you want. Use your Shadow learning, the Life Areas, your Hot Spots, the chakras, something you learned on your trip, something you learned in the last experiment, something that just happened this morning. You choose.

The main idea?

Lay it all out there and do everyone on the planet a favor, including you: choose big.

1) Rank It:

To begin this experiment, pause a moment to ponder complete fulfillment—bliss-filled even.

What if, on a scale from 1-10, your life was a 10?

Or a 20?

Wanna go really big? Go for 100.

What's the number that makes you gulp and grin? That's a fun place to begin.

Write your number here:

2) (En)vision It:

Next, close your eyes and imagine whatever it is you want to do or be or wear or feel in this ideal life. See, smell, taste, hear, sense every part. Embody it. Get it in your sights. Stay with the vision as long as you like. Then, notice that bliss, breathe into it and when you're ready, **open up and write about it until you've covered every detail, front and back:**

2a) Done writing? Nope:

Reeeeally imagine those kick-ass intentions. Think bigger. Bolder. Envision everything you've always wanted. Write your best life. In full color. In total detail. **Keep it going:**

3) Bring Back the Magic Spell:

There. NOW you have your vision. And you're ready to bring it to life. A great place to start? Your Be, Do, Know magic spell.

Be:
Take note of your being when you ponder your vision: what comes up? Feel this sensation. This giddiness. This excitement. (Oops! Feeling fear arise? That's OK. Experience it, let it move through you, then get back into your wonderful, dream life. Don't worry about how you'll make it happen yet, just feel it; just be your vision in your mind.)

Do:
Next, allow that possibility-rich being to move you into action and guide your doing. Notice opportunities for creating your ideal vision right now in your life. Whether it's giant leaps or baby steps, what will bring you closer to your vision? What can you do?

Know:
Now, take all this learning and make a commitment to yourself to take at least one action or think one new thought or reach out to one new person that will alert the universe that you are serious about this new life. Something to help you begin to see, experience and know this new journey. Put it in writing to make it official.

Hey Universe! I'm ready. To prove it to you, I make this commitment to myself:

4) Finally, Tap the Power of Now:

Lastly, as you move through this Vision Quest, you'll notice that it's sorta like goal setting. And sorta not.

Here's the difference: With a Vision Quest, your focus is on the only space where anything ever happens. The now.

So, check out the following ideas to keep your vision front and center, illustrating your commitment to living with courage, possibility and choice in the now.

Create a Soul Collage:
The next generation of the old-school Vision Board, Soul Collages are more abstract. To create one, sit for a bit and listen to your soul. Consider those essential aspects of You that want to come out to play. Then, grab some old magazines and look for photos that capture the feeling of your vision—not stuff, but sensations. (Get back in your being space for inspiration!) Cut and paste your pics on piece of tag board in a collage. Place it somewhere noticeable. Ta-daa. Internal intentions set. Now feel that you ARE this energy and, well, you know the rest.

Mindmap It:
A Soul Collage for word hounds, a Mindmap is a word collage that helps you to break a big picture into comfortable chunks. All so you can start taking action. On a blank sheet of paper, write your vision in the middle. Place branches out from the center to represent various aspects of what your vision means to you. Branch off from there as you capture more important words and phrases. Place your Mindmap somewhere noticeable. Use it to provide you with direction as you begin to manifest your vision.

Create a Trophy Song List:

Music brings out emotions, takes us on journeys and, when living in choice, a good song has the power to inspire and/or kick us in the butt. Here's an easy one: Put your playlist on shuffle, ask a question in relation to your vision before each song, get a radical answer. Or: Create your very own Vision Mix. Listen daily for inspiration. And don't forget to dance.

Write an Aliveness Manifesto:

A manifesto is nothing more than a written declaration of principles, beliefs and objectives. Explore the principles and beliefs you hold about your vision. Remember: you are not only Editor-in-Chief of your life, you are also the top dog, CEO, ruler and ultimate leader. So, what's your public declaration? How will you lead an alive life? What does that entail? Write it down. Post it proudly. Read it aloud. Feel it come alive.

Life Map. Revisited. Again:

Another great tool for vision creation is to revisit the original Life Map from the Prep section. With your new vision in mind, complete the Map again with one key difference: Ask yourself not what your life looks like now, but what you would like it to look like in the future—you know, bliss-filled and infused with aliveness. Write down your desired Level of Aliveness in each Life Area (10? 50? 100?!) and create intentions for it right now.

Insert-Your-Idea-Here:

What else could you create that illustrates your choice to live in the now? A sculpture? A blog? A business plan? A latch-hook rug?! Whatever inspires you to keep the power of choice active in your space, in your mind and in your life, have at it. **It's your vision.**

[RE-ENTRY] Baggage Buster Redux

"There's a crack in everything, that's how the light gets in."

–Leonard Cohen

Uh-oh. What's *that?!*

You've aced the flow of Courage, Possibility and Choice. You're back in the vibe of Be, Do, Know. You've created the Vision of all Visions. You're well on your way to complete and utter aliveness in your everyday life.

Until: BAM!

Where'd that baggage come from?!

"What's this ickiness? Why do I feel so cranky? Why is my baggage sneaking up and blind-siding me at this lovely restaurant / during this meeting / in this chat with my partner? What's happening?!"

No worries. No judgment. No problem.

Evolution is a process that takes unexpected detours and reroutes.

At times it's quite surprising.

And just when you think you have it down, a challenge appears.

So, when that crusty baggage shows up, it helps to remember that we're all just practicing at life. It's normal and expected to have many opportunities to learn, unlearn and re-learn. It's called growth. And it takes time.

Think of it as a trip to the gym. It's your aliveness workout.

Just like you don't expect to be physically buff after five sit-ups, becoming metaphysically buff is a process, too. When transforming our lives, many successful reps of new thoughts and behaviors are required to help remove old barriers. Toning takes effort. Shedding old habits is a commitment. So, be kind to yourself.

And when old baggage shows up, remember this:

The goal of aliveness is to remain flexible and moving with the flow.

Not stuck.

Not rut-pulled.

Not hooked on old stories or habits that serve an old you.

As long as what you're doing continues to serve an alive and evolving you, you're rocking, you're rolling, you're embarking on a major shift of gigantic proportions.

The good news?

Most of the time, this should feel (relatively) great.

But, those other times? Those tougher times? Those I'm-really-not-interested times?

Try this instead:

> • BE assured that you have all the power in the universe right there in your incredible heart.
> • DO the very thing that allows this being to shine as brightly as possible.
> • And KNOW that you choose how you want to live. Every. Single. Moment. Every. Single. Day.

As Paulo Coelho tells us:

"You drown not by falling into a river, but by staying submerged in it."

So, if you fall, get back up.

Climb out of the damn river.

Explore your courage to keep on learning.

Stay committed to all the possibilities that exist.

Explore the choices that lead you to new lessons, new knowledge and a new point of power to choose yet again.

This adventure—your life—doesn't have time for self-flagellation or victim talk.

Your life wants you in the driver's seat.

Your life wants you to hold the reins.

Your life wants you to lead the way.

And that's the truth.

[RE-ENTRY] Practice Makes Powerful

"We must give ourselves permission to act out our dreams and visions, not look for more sensations, more phenomena, but live our strongest dreams—even if it takes a lifetime."

–Vijali Hamilton

Live it, learn it, love it.

By now, you've really opened up. You've played with experiments that pushed your boundaries and introduced new options. You've created an amazing vision and are committed to achieving your dreams. You've bravely approached your baggage and are equipped to begin to choose anew.

Now, get ready for the final experiments to bring it all home.

It's time for new ways to infuse ongoing aliveness into your world. Long-view exercises to integrate into your daily routine. Passionate ideas to make every day as luscious and joyful and adventurous as your best day away.

Practice makes perfect?

Nah. With e>v, practice makes powerful.

Let's do this!

Grrr-atitude Revisited

When traveling, it's so easy to appreciate every moment exploring, every moment spent with loved ones, every moment on vacation. Now, back at home, what if this level of appreciation was all around you? And you simply hadn't noticed it?

Yep, gratitude: the gift that keeps on giving.

We spoke in Prep about the wonderfully obnoxious practice of gratitude and how it has the power to unlock the fullness of life.

Even more, many studies have been done about the benefits of saying thank you, from enhanced relationships to better health. (It feels good AND it's good for you? What could be better than that?)

So, try it out. Right here. Right now. Take a moment and look around and...

Name three things that you are grateful for right now, and why:

1)

2)

3)

Now, isn't that a beautiful dose of joy?! Even more, what if you made that a practice? In the morning. In the moment. At the end of each day. **Give thanks.**

Elevating the Mundane

Along the lines of gratitude: you know how, on vacation, even the most mundane of items or experiences are somehow more? An antique spoon at a quaint cafe suddenly isn't just a spoon. A glance through a 150-year-old windowpane isn't just a view of the street. We cherish what comes from afar and, once home again, we often get dulled by the familiar.

Instead: Is there a way to give each life gesture the value it deserves? To elevate your morning shower to a spa-worthy moment? To elevate your mid-day coffee break from a rushed to-go cup to a quiet break for an espresso in a real, porcelain demitasse? To elevate your evening dinner plans from the standard take-out menu to a restaurant you've never tried, or a cuisine you've never experimented with? **Look around, what deserves some elevation?**

Rituals and Reminders

On vacation, rituals are everywhere. The flourish of meticulously packing every item. The fanfare of that first "We're on vacation!" toast. The seeking, finding, recapping and retelling with travel mates. All rooted in the core idea of excitedly exploring.

And at home? Rituals can be personalized, simple actions taken on a regular basis. All to remind you of important aspects of your vision and aliveness. To keep the energy front and center.

Ideas: Take time every day to zone into vacation mode; simply stop and consciously see, hear, feel, taste or smell your surroundings as if you were there for the first time. (Set an alarm on your phone or reminder on your calendar.) Create a daily "top three favorite things that happened today" list; share every night over dinner. (Keep this journal going.) Take a midday walk to think about nothing other than that very moment. (Do it now.)

Ready to create your own ritual? What will you do to bring aliveness into your life?

What are the best habits you want to bring in to your daily experience?

What is the one thing you are motivated to add to or remove from your day that will make the biggest difference?

How will you remind yourself every day of the good you want to create?

What represents the idea of aliveness to you: a place, a photo, a sentiment, a person? Who or what will help and support you?

How will you remember to get back on the aliveness track if you stumble? Remember, it's ALL learning. You fall down, you get back up. It's that simple.

Body Talk

When on vacation, we often turn off our head and let our body lead the way. We kick off our shoes and sink our toes into the sand. We feel the breeze on our skin. We taste food fully. We stop to smell the roses.

In Re-Entry, what about checking in with your body to see what it has to tell you? We mentioned the chakras as a tuning fork. This can be a great place to revisit today and every day. Try this:

Sit a moment and just breathe.

Where do you notice your energy freely flowing? Where might there be blocks? (Scratchy throat inhibiting expression? Upset stomach testifying an abundance of stress? Or: butterflies in your tummy pointing to playful excitement? Joyful swelling in your chest indicating your great big compassion for the world around you?)

What sorts of clues does your body give you? Where are you noticing connections, literal or metaphorical? In the Life Areas? Where does that point you?

What do the chakras or colors bring into this scan? Do you find yourself drawn to and/or wearing a lot of a particular color lately? What's that about?

What if you flipped it and surrounded yourself with a particular color to energize a Life Area or region of the body? What's there?

On Path

When traveling, we're often tuned into the path of least resistance. We allow ourselves to go with the flow. When we get back home, however, it sometimes feels like we're swimming against the current. A good practice?

Find your *Desire Path*.

According to Wikipedia: "A Desire Path is created as a consequence of erosion caused by foot-fall or traffic. The path usually represents the shortest or most easily navigated route between an origin and destination."

Essentially, a Desire Path is the natural place that people walk to get from point A to point B. The interesting thing: in our ordered world, a Desire Path isn't always where the sidewalk is.

In fact, more enlightened architects and planners sometimes wait to lay pavement or cement within a park or campus, to see how and where people naturally travel from place to place. Then, once the paths are evident, a more permanent solution is applied. Try this same idea with your life.

Which paths are you following simply because they're already paved?

What if you rerouted?

Where's the shortcut? Or the scenic view?

How can you experiment with new directions before setting things in stone?

Where is a new path of least resistance?

Downsize to Live Large

On vacation, one can travel quite far with only a few items at the ready. What about bringing that lightness home? From decluttering and death cleaning to the tiny house movement and minimalism, many people are enjoying the financial and, even, health benefits of living with less.

Think back to that unfettered feeling of vacation and ask yourself:

What feels good about traveling light?

Do I need all this house or all this stuff? What's the quantity vs. quality quotient?

What's my attachment to or relationship with things?

What if I lived with fewer items, but created more memories?

What would that feel like? Financially? Emotionally?

Creating the Pause

Pausing—taking that moment to simply admire a view, taking a break to inhale the present moment, taking a beat to tune into your travel mate (or yourself!)—is abundant on vacation. But when we get back home? We're multi-tasking. We're cooking on all burners. We're zoom, zoom, zooming through life. All at the speed of light.

Idea: Use some of the breathwork sequences from the Trip or explore an expanded practice to build this proactively into your day. Want guidance and support here? Try out a local meditation center or check out the many mindfulness apps that exist.

Even more? Integrating mindful moments into your day—creating multiple, intentional pauses—is another idea. Mindful moments help you notice when you're driven by to-do lists or when baggage might be lurking about. In essence, they help you notice where you're at and what you're up to. And that puts you back in the driver seat and back in choice. (And, yes, there's an app for that, too!)

To get started, ask yourself:

Where can I allow more pauses and mindful moments during my day?

How will pausing refresh me?

What stories do I have about pausing? About taking a break? About stopping to appreciate the moment or to be present?

When can I start?

What can I do?

Being With What Is

On vacation, not only are we awesomely aware of our surroundings, but we also often accept the world and all its beautiful flaws, quirks and hiccups with open acceptance.

We let things slide.

We go with the flow.

We gleefully live by the immortal words of Jimmy Buffett: "If life gives you limes, make margaritas."

In short: we accept things as they are because, what do we care? We're on vacation!

But, when we're back home? Oof.

Acceptance can be big challenge.

From daily inconveniences of traffic jams to big life-changes like losing a job, acceptance is a huge continuum.

Some things we can accept freely, with shoulders shrugged. Others we resist and rage against with fists of full-on fury. Even more, we often confuse acceptance with agreement. AKA, if we're not railing against all of the atrocities, large or small, in the world, are we saying we are OK with them? (The answer is "no," by the way.)

Instead, in her book *Radical Acceptance*, Buddhist Tara Brach offers the idea that acceptance is nothing more than: "the willingness to experience ourselves and our lives as it is."

In short: Life happens. Period.

The good, the bad, the ugly, the light and, you got it, the Shadow.

Or, when we can experience ourselves as we are, in all of our human messiness, with all of our imperfections...

And, when we can experience our lives as they are, constantly changing, always transforming, ever new...

We then open ourselves to a whole new world of options, possibilities and magic.

So, ask yourself:

Where in my life can I bring in more acceptance?

How can I show up differently?

Is there a new way to approach my life, or a long-standing irritation or a new transformation with a more open and accepting—a vacation—heart or mind?

Brach also posits, "The boundary to what we can accept is the boundary to our freedom." Ask yourself: where's my boundary of acceptance? Of my freedom?

We're All In This Together

You know that feeling on vacation.

When it's so easy to connect with strangers, locals, plane-mates, fellow SCUBA divers, you name it. When it's so easy to show your exuberance, to be excited about the world, to be an active participant in it. When it's even easy to make mistakes or an innocent, cultural faux pas or to try to communicate with only hand signals or smiles or laughter.

With an open heart and mind, connecting with the world is so joyful. And easy.

But once you're home? Fears kick in, public mistakes aren't allowed and playing it cool is everything.

Not anymore.

Remember: you are an integral player on this planet. Your interaction and uniqueness—these things matter; what you share with the world matters. In short, without you, this world would not be the same.

So, as you settle into Re-Entry, keep your vacation-y, childlike, visible wonder for the world alive.

As you do, you may notice that when you choose to share this level of aliveness, people in your circle may react differently to you.

Some may distance themselves: that's OK, they're on their own path.

Also, others might take on a new significance to you: that's great, you're attracting people who are on the same wavelength, literally and figuratively.

Either way, on your aliveness journey, you'll soon find that it's really helpful to have a community of supporters, encouragers and cheerleaders to remind you of how wonderful you really are. And to remind them of the same.

So, as with everything else, you get to choose.

On your journey into aliveness, who will you surround yourself with?

Who is in your tribe?

Old or new, current stranger or trusted confidante, who do you want in your life?

Remember: no need for judgment here.

No need for *don't wants* to take the stage; that doesn't tell anyone—including you—what you *do* want.

Instead, to begin imagining your ideal tribe, write down your perfect group of friends, co-workers, family, whomever you want to surround you on this journey.

It can be specific people.

It can be qualities you want to experience in people.

It can be experiences you want to have with people.

Even more, it can be who you'll be when you're around this enlightened group of individuals.

Take a moment to play with the questions below, brainstorm and—yes!—write it all down to make it real.

As you step into aliveness, who will you surround yourself with?

What awesome traits do these people have?

How, in turn, will you shine your light and be an inspiration to others?

What is the essence of your tribe or group?

And, together, how will you help transform the world?

NAV TIP: BE THE CHANGE
Remember the age-old wisdom: "Like attracts like."

Or, as Gandhi said: "Be the change you wish to see in the world."

In other words, in order to attract amazing people to you, you have to be and do amazing things yourself.

So, don't forget to ponder who you'll be and what you'll do to attract your new tribe.

Practice allowing your being to guide your doing every day. And watch as you begin to meet—and know—all sorts of amazing people.

P.S. They're waiting to know you, too.

———

Finally: It's Vacation. Every Day.

One last "Practice Makes Powerful" thought?

One more insight?

One final reminder?

All along this entire journey, every experiment you've played with, every question you've answered, every idea you've pondered is based on one, core truth:

***Evolution Through Vacation* works no matter where you are.**

Yep, it's true.

From creating a Life Map to recording Morning Meds to gathering Evening Impressions to Tripping Up Your Trip to checking your everyday baggage, the experiments in e>v can be used and re-used no matter if you're on the road or not.

Ideas:

> **• What if your read this book from the very beginning through the lens of your everyday vacation—your life?**

> **• What if you lived in adventure right now?**

> **• What if you followed the entire e>v process and never left home?**

> **• Or, what if you picked up a travel guide for your city and enjoyed the cool things that make up the space you live in every day?**

> **• What if you saw your city through the eyes of a visitor? What does it look like?**

> **• What if you experienced your life with the eyes of a traveler? What does it look like?**

There's adventure to be had right outside your front door. Every single day.

Find it.

[RE-ENTRY] The Aliveness Movement

"Now is the only time. How we relate to it creates the future. In other words, if we're going to be more cheerful in the future, it's because of our aspiration and exertion to be cheerful in the present. What we do accumulates; the future is the result of what we do right now."

—Pema Chödrön

So, that's it.

That's *Evolution Through Vacation.*

Got it?

Ready to go?

Equipped to live in the present?

Excited to blaze new trails and venture down new roads?

Energized to live a liminal, in-the-moment, alive life?

Well, then, get out there and be brilliant.

Be inspired.

Be courageous.

Be You.

And as you continue to evolve and change and grow, as you and your tribe share your gifts with the world, as you inspire others to live just as fully, remember:

Every day holds the gift of courage if you allow to receive it.

Every day brings the possibility of aliveness if you allow it to appear.

And every day is a vacation day if you choose it to be.

This is the journey called life.

Everyone has the passport.

Everyone has the right to explore.

Everyone belongs here.

And everyone has the choice—the exquisite, awesome, beautiful choice—to make it the best trip it can be.

Thank you for bringing yourself to the adventure.

So, what's next?

[EXTRAS]

[EXTRAS] In Gratitude

We shall not cease from exploration
And the end
Of all our exploring
Will be to arrive where we started
And know the place for the first time.

—T.S. Eliot

This is a story about old friends. And new beginnings.

In August of 2005, after years of moving and traveling and jobs and relationships, three friends from college—Keri, Gretchen and Elissa—made a date to catch up.

In line with the energy of our connection, we chose to celebrate our long-time bond by attending a concert by one of Keri's favorite foot-stomping, glass-raising, global bands.

It was fabulous.

On the night of the show, the three of us had a kick-ass time dancing and laughing and toasting and hooting and hollering all through the concert.

And, in our revelry and music-induced glee, we vividly imagined us all on a road trip together, seeing a show out of town and letting the adventure unfold.

We all loved the music! And each other! And travel! So, it was decided: We would simply spend more time out in the world dancing and laughing and toasting and hooting and hollering. And we would hit the road. Together.

The universe, of course, had other plans.

Not even one month later, on September 22, 2005, our beloved, inspirational, crazy, beautiful friend Keri had an allergic reaction to an antibiotic, fell into a coma and died.

Just. Like. That.

After much shock, grieving and contemplating we, Gretchen and Elissa, bonded together stronger than ever with the hopes of moving through our pain as well as finding a way to commemorate and celebrate this incredible woman.

Though it took time, a memory started to appear and the sun started to come out.

When spring hinted at blossoming, we suddenly began to emerge as well. We began to be able to embrace Keri's *life* again: her spirit and enthusiasm and, among other amazing gifts, her incredible passion for music and travel.

The obvious choice? Honor Keri with joyful exploration and get out there in the world to dance and laugh and toast and hoot and holler. Just as we'd planned.

So, we hit the road for a spring tour, visiting cities and attending shows by none other than Keri's favorite band.

Little did we know of the transformation that would occur as a result.

On the road, we allowed these vacations, these adventures, to open ourselves up to experiences reminiscent of our friend's intense, joyful spirit and vibrant manner of engaging with the world.

In the space of tribute and daring, we allowed synchronicity and magic to enter. We threw away outmoded expectations of ourselves and old stories about who we were or could be. We exorcised old demons and sent them scurrying. We believed in our beauty and strength; trusted and challenged each other; took a leap into the flow of the Universe.

And it was on one of these trips that the phrase "Evolution Through Vacation" first appeared.

It was right on. "Evolution Through Vacation" (or "e-through-v" as we started to call it) was the perfect descriptor for both the space we created and the change we embraced.

Especially, because, that spring we didn't travel far. The places we landed were not exotic nor all that foreign. And that became the point.

Our physical location had become truly secondary to the transformation afoot all around and within us. The places didn't matter; the journey within mattered. And that's what changed everything.

As we learned and explored living in this moment, we soon came to realize that we couldn't keep all this goodness for ourselves. And, in fact, in sharing this with others, the goodness would grow exponentially.

And so, e>v was born.

A perfect way to honor a woman as joyful and daring as our friend Keri.

So, thank you, Keri, for your gracious spirit. Your winks and nods. Your always-frank and refreshing world-view. And for the courage to ask and answer tough questions about what it really means to be alive. Much love, girlfriend. You continue to change the world with the gifts you have shared.

To the aliveness adventure,
Gretchen & Elissa

[EXTRAS] Resources

"Be yourself; everyone else is already taken."

—Oscar Wilde

Our go-to inspiration group? People who enlighten and enthuse?

Here's a starter list of folks who've inspired this book, our work and our lives; people we've also referenced within.

Google their names. Find their books, theories and websites and support their work. Then, create your own masterpiece. Share your own philosophy. And keep the aliveness magic alive!

- **Howard Thurman**
- **Christine McDougall**
- **Mary Oliver**
- **Geoffrey F. Abert**
- **Michael Franti**
- **Jason Mraz**
- **Yung Pueblo**
- **Ralph Waldo Emerson**
- **Henry David Thoreau**
- **Norman Vincent Peale**
- **Alexander Graham Bell**
- **Anaïs Nin**
- **Chögyam Trungpa Rinpoche**
- **Arnold Van Gennep**
- **Victor Turner**

- **Joseph Campbell**
- **Wayne Dyer**
- **Julia Cameron**
- **Melody Beattie**
- **Ernest Holmes**
- **A.C. Ping**
- **Brené Brown**
- **Gregg Braden**
- **Debbie Ford**
- **Yoda**
- **Kobi Yamada**
- **Danny Kaye**
- **Gilda Radner**
- **The Dalai Lama**
- **Albert Ellis**
- **Tom Stoppard**
- **Carl Sagan**
- **Glennon Doyle Melton**
- **Albert Einstein**
- **Earl Nightingale**
- **Cecil Beaton**
- **Nelson Mandela**
- **Thich Nhat Hanh**
- **Ambrose Redmoon**
- **James Hollis**
- **Carl Jung**
- **Jacob Nordby**
- **Vasant Lad**
- **Vicki Howie**
- **Ernest Holmes**
- **Leonard Cohen**
- **Tara Brach**
- **Paulo Coelho**
- **Vijali Hamilton**
- **Oscar Wilde**

Thanks to Freepik for the cover art. And a special shout-out to Dr. Karen Mattison for putting the cherry on this galactic sundae.

Gretchen Carlson

Wanderer. Wonderer. Adventurer. Listener. Laugher. Love junkie. Happy paddler. Guerrilla gardener. Dancer. Raven-spired. Pearl.

As a life coach, teacher and trainer over the past few decades, Gretchen's been blessed to work with folks who want to heal their hearts, access their mojo, up their game, tap into the mystery. However they name it, it's all to uncover and live their fullest, deepest, most enlivened selves. Every day.

Out in the world, Gretchen is happiest:

- Listening to live music anywhere, any time
- Discovering hidden places
- Circled round the fire with friends
- Sitting breathing
- On the road

Gretchen lives with her partner & puppy in the peaks & valleys of Montana.

Elissa Gjertson

Experimenter. Explorer. Pattern seeker. Idea generator. Yoga lover. Street photographer. Island hopper. Inventor. Maker. Expat.

Elissa is a transformation-obsessed writer and entrepreneur. In addition to e>v, she loves to inspire and empower employees and org change leaders at frankitchangekit.com, curate DIY cabin style at cabinspiration.com and upcycle furniture & other goods in her backyard studio.

Out in the world, Elissa is happiest:

- Just when the plane takes off
- Scouring alley markets for vintage fabric or furniture
- Finding the oldest bar/restaurant in town
- Hanging with friends & family
- Near water

Elissa lives with her husband on the island of Java, Indonesia.

CPSIA information can be obtained
at www.ICGtesting.com
Printed in the USA
FSHW02n1517290518
48637FS